Grand Wok Cookbook

Olivia Wu

BARRON'S

Woodbury, New York • London • Toronto • Sydney

All inquiries should be addressed to:
Barron's Educational Series, Inc.
113 Crossways Park Drive
Woodbury, New York 11797

International Standard Book No. 0-8120-5593-4
Library of Congress Catalog Card No. 84-12331

Library of Congress Cataloging in Publication Data
Wu, Olivia.
  The grand wok cookbook.

  Includes index.
  1. Wok cookery. I. Title.
TX840.W65W8 1984   641.5'89   · 84-12331
ISBN 0-8120-5593-4

PRINTED IN THE UNITED STATES OF AMERICA

4 5 6 7   880   9 8 7 6 5 4 3 2 1

Photographic Credits

Color photography by Matthew Klein
Yoshiko Loomis, food stylist
Linda Cheverton, prop stylist

Accessories courtesy of the following: China by Fitz and Floyd (available through Bloomingdales, New York); sterling silver flatware from Georg Jenson Silversmiths, New York; sterling silver bowl and serving pieces from Buccellati Silver, New York; sterling silver chopstick rests and silver-tipped chopsticks from Buccellati, New York; handthrown cobalt blue porcelain plate and antique blue and white platter from Gordon Foster, New York; flowers from Very Special Flowers, New York.

Jacket and cover design Milton Glaser, Inc.
Book design Milton Glaser, Inc.

Contents

Introduction

Take everything from me but one good knife, a source of intense heat, and my wok—and I'd still be happy. Send me, armed with a wok and a knife, to a desert island—or even the heart of Paris—and I'd continue to cook and eat in bliss.

A cook can do a million and one things in a wok: poach a whole fish, whip up an omelette, fry a chicken, roast chestnuts, make the *roux* for a sauce, steam appetizer dumplings, cook a stew, fry rice, sear a filet mignon . . . and so on. The wok is the universal cooking pan *par excellence.*

In Shanghai, where I was born, I saw the woks set over charcoal braziers in the streets alongside store entrances and sidewalk homes. A mother would squat beside the wok, quickly tossing and stirring up the dishes of an entire meal for her family of eight. Elsewhere in the city, in the kitchens of classy restaurants, each chef could count row upon row of woks to himself. A chef presides over the burners flaming at a volcanic 25,000 BTUs, a wok on each burner. He dances from one wok mixture to the next. All four limbs are called into use. The knees control the switches, the arms toss and stir and shake while flashes of steel and iron spark the air.

Visit any stall or sidewalk cafe-type restaurant in Hong Kong or places up and down the China coast. Order the house specialty and then watch the cook prime the propane tank, heat the wok, and conjure up an oyster crêpe, stir-fried noodles with shrimp, or an omelette with crabmeat. The wok is the world's most efficient frying pan, and the most efficient pan or pot overall. No other cooking utensil gives the cook more fun or a greater sense of exuberance. And it cooks every ingredient under the sun.

The wok leads you naturally and automatically toward cooking as a 60-minute gourmet—often in less than 60 minutes. It is a friend to help you create hearty and speedy meals in one pot, without sacrificing the opportunity to cook impressively or to entertain with gusto. Look at its soft but dynamic design and note how its features work for you:

> *The wok is big—the more room for you to toss and stir without inhibition. Its roominess is not meant to be filled. Think instead that it is a large salad bowl, with room to toss.*
>
> *The wok is round—the more to help quicken the turning of the ingredients for uniform mixing. Its hemispheric shape accelerates the speed of the ingredients as they race around the curves of the wok.*

*The wok is deep—*the more to maximize and control your use of oil. With less oil than it takes to coat a skillet, you can stir-fry quickly; with much less oil than it takes to fill a deep-fryer, you can deep-fry to a golden crispness. The wok is also deep enough for braising.*

*The wok is high—*used with its lid, the wok has sufficient space to allow steam to rise and gently cook foods. Wok-steaming is a wonderful alternative to drier oven heating and reheating.*

The wok is a brilliant compromise of a flat and a deep pan. Cooking in it is a joy and a wonder to learn, and it opens up the doors to the art of cooking. The wok can liberate you to all styles of food. Don't limit yourself to Asian cuisine with the wok. The pleasure and ease which come with its use will start you on your way to the foods of other nationalities, maybe eventually to your own innovative cookery. Enjoy the adventures to which it leads you!

ACKNOWLEDGMENTS

I thank my family of friends who have helped at every stage of this book, from culinary to print and from hand-holding to babysitting. It is no coincidence that, with these same people, I can always share table, conversation, and laughter. I thank my husband, Calvin, for providing encouragement, challenge, and solitude; and my son Erling (born the day before the book) for providing none of these but for simply and intensely being himself.

Special thanks are due to Brian Victor, who assisted me with the recipes in the entire book, and Sandy Leach, who assisted in past cooking classes, scrubbed pots, and read recipes; and with whom I enjoy sharing kitchen space. Finally I thank Judith Olney, unique and impressive among cook-authors, and my editor, Carole Berglie, who did a great volume of editing in very little time, and helped me re-shape the manuscript and the recipes.

This book is dedicated to my mother in loving memory.

How to Use This Book

If you've used a wok before, you recognize that a certain ease and flow accompany cooking in a wok. Speed is a major component in mastering its use and in producing the type of clean, natural, lightly cooked foods which often earmark wok cookery. Your motions need not be frantic, but you must organize the sequence of events, much as a director orders the scenes of a play. The actors—or, in this case, your ingredients—are costumed and made up ahead of time, and can enter and exit the stage—or the wok—with ease.

This is why the recipes in this book follow a format different from most other cookbooks. It has been designed especially for stir-frying because this manner of cooking makes pressing demands on your organizational and timing skills. The format has worked well with my students, and I hope it will work for you too. It has been dubbed a sort of "flow chart," and I hope you will use it to create a flow of movements as you work with your wok.

THE RECIPE FORMAT

You'll note that the recipes follow generally a two-column format. The left-hand column presents the shorthand—an overview of the whole recipe—while the right-hand side gives detailed descriptions and instructions. I suggest that you first read the whole recipe, going across the page first noting the left-hand side for the general description and ingredients needed, then moving across the page to the corresponding instructions on the right-hand side. As you become familiar with the recipes and with the methods of wok cooking, you may forego looking at the right-hand side because you will be familiar with the techniques. Eventually you may not need to look at the recipe at all, because you will automatically organize your tasks to the left column of your mind. The Chinese never use a recipe when cooking in a wok because they are able to place mentally each ingredient in its proper sequence before they cook.

Time and Measurement: These elements are embodied in the left-hand column. Run your eye down this column of a recipe and you will get an idea of how long the preparation will take. I avoid putting down exact times because they tend to be frustrating and misleading; each cook knows how long it takes him or her to chop, slice, or grind; and unlike most ovens, stovetop temperatures vary considerably from home to home. Most cookbooks reflect the speed of the author, who can be faster than the average cook, and the efficiency of professional equipment, which tend to be hotter. We are individuals with varied abilities and tools, and only you can best estimate how long it will take you to cut broccoli or heat oil.

Measurements are given for ingredients, but in most instances you need not follow them exactly. The wok implies economy of food. It can also imply economy of time and motion, and economy of equipment. Don't fumble around with a measuring spoon while stir-frying. If you must measure exactly, do so before you begin cooking. But, better yet, learn the measures of your wok tools, and approximate your ingredients. Pour oil into your spatula and measure it for future use. Mine holds 1½ tablespoons of liquid, and I use that quicker measuring device as I cook. Many Chinese cooks continue to measure this way. Also, you may ruin a dish by overcooking it if you take the time to measure things with a spoon. You certainly will ruin the freedom and fun of wok cooking, as well as cut down on the efficiency. (Other suggestions for measuring are given on pages 23–24 and in the chapter on stir-fry techniques.)

Details and Explanations: The right-hand column holds all the information that cannot fit into the left column with regard to preparing the ingredients for cooking and then cooking itself. In this part of the recipe I often describe how things should be cut, or how long they should be marinated. I describe what you should see, smell, feel, or taste to judge if the dish is done or if it is ready for the next ingredient. And when necessary I give you the approximate cooking times, particularly if the dish or technique is unfamiliar.

IMPROVISATION

For some recipes to have truly successful results—complex recipes, desserts and recipes new to you—follow the instructions exactly, using the measurements indicated. In many other instances, however, you are invited to adjust seasonings to your taste, to add or subtract elements as you prefer, perhaps even to eventually direct your own combinations. Those recipes for which exact measurements are necessary have been keyed in this book with a footnote; for all others, the options are open.

Remember, however, that improvisation cannot be taught. It comes from first acquiring a sense of taste and proportion, and knowing the raw ingredients with which you work. It also comes from a thorough knowledge of wok cooking—a process you must absorb through to your bones. I suggest you learn to use the wok—in all its facets—and follow the recipes in this book. Then wean yourself of them and also of the worn-out recipes you know too well. Try new elements, add new ingredients within the prescribed guidelines, but use the techniques you have learned and mastered well. A Chinese cook rarely creates a new dish because the traditional ones are so satisfying, but he or she feels a certain freedom within the formulas. That Chinese cook sticks to the technical procedures and just changes the acceptable ingredients—with infinite results. It is basically the same play, but with new characters who interact with different results. This is the way to knowledgeable, liberated, and joyful wok cooking.

Cooking with the Wok

A Pictorial Guide to Assorted Techniques and Terminology

1

2

3

The wok is a big, round, deep cooking surface with high sides. It is a brilliant compromise of a flat and a deep pan. Don't reserve your wok for just oriental dishes; use it to prepare your Western foods as well, following basic wok techniques.

STIR-FRYING

The most common type of wok cooking, stir-frying is the quick cooking of uniformly sized ingredients in a small quantity of hot oil, with the wok set over high heat. For a detailed explanation of stir-fry, see pages 3–12. Here are the steps to follow in making a basic stir-fry.

1. Heat wok until hot. Add oil according to your recipe and allow the oil to heat until almost smoking. Add garlic, scallion, or ginger and render in hot oil, then remove and discard.

2. Add seasoned meat and toss it around in the wok, almost as if you were tossing a salad, until the shreds separate and the color of the meat changes.

3. Scoop out the meat and juices with your spatula and place on a platter (1). Clean wok and put back on heat. Add a little more oil when wok is hot again.

4. Add the green peppers and bamboo shoots, and toss in the wok for a few minutes (2). Do not overcook. Keep the vegetables moving in the hot oil until their fragrance and some liquid are released — they should be cooked, but remain crisp and bright.

5. Return the meat to the wok (3) and combine-fry until all ingredients are thoroughly heated. Give the mixture several turns, and remove from the heat to serve.

Some Special Tips

Have your ingredients cut to similar shapes and equal sizes, ready for stir-frying. Just before stir-frying, arrange them on a board or plate alongside your stove.

Add your ingredients quickly, pouring in the entire item all at once. Don't drop the pieces into the wok individually; use your spatula, if necessary, to push them off the plate quickly.

Pour in your seasoning or thickening mixture at the end. The gravy thickener should be pre-mixed and ready. Re-stir the mixture just before adding, to be certain all the starch is dissolved in the liquid.

Other Wok Techniques

STEAMING

Many of the dishes in this book use steaming as the means of cooking (see pages 13–15). Put the food to be steamed on a plate that will fit atop a steaming rack which can be placed in the wok. Arrange the food in a single layer, and then bring the water in the wok to a full boil before placing in the plate of food. Put heat to level indicated in the recipe, and cover wok. The food will be cooked gently, as the steam swirls up and around the dish.

For most foods, it is recommended that you use a steaming dish and place it on the rack for steaming. In some instances — for example, to steam dumplings — it is preferable to place the food directly on the steaming rack. In these cases, use a stacking bamboo or rattan steamer. Brush the steamer with a little oil, then place the food in the steamer basket and cover with lid.

BRAISING OR POACHING

You can use your wok in much the same manner as you would a Dutch oven or large casserole, although the food will cook a little faster and you must be a little more careful to monitor the level of the cooking liquid.

When braising, first fry the meat in the wok to brown the outside, then add liquid to cover. Add any desired seasonings, such as scallions, ginger, or sherry, and bring liquid to a boil. Reduce heat, cover, and simmer until done.

1

2

3

DEEP-FRYING

The wok is excellent for deep-frying because the oil is deep enough to submerge the food while wide enough to maneuver it about. You will also use less oil when deep-frying in a wok than in a standard deep-fryer.

Add enough oil to wok, depending on what you are frying, and heat it to at least 350 degrees, or the temperature indicated in your recipe. Ease the food into the hot oil and turn to cook both sides. Fry only small amounts of food at one time, since too large a batch will lower the temperature of the oil too much. Scoop out your deep-fried food when done and drain on a paper towel.

Sometimes, a whole fish or chicken is immersed in oil to be deep-fried. For example, prepare a fish for deep-frying according to your recipe, then lifting the fish by its tail, slide it into the hot oil (1).

Continuously bathe the fish with the hot oil, especially any portions not covered with the oil in the wok (2).

Put the spatula underneath the fish and hold the fish in the center of the top with chopsticks (3). Turn over and deep-fry on other side, then drain and transfer fish to a serving platter.

Photographs in this pictorial guide are from *Chinese Cooking for Two* by Nancy Chih Ma, reprinted courtesy of Kodansha Ltd.

The Technique of Stir-frying

When Chinese cooks tell each other their recipes, a dance takes place. First, a few hand movements. Then the gestures grow bigger. Animation increases until the hips twitch. What are they describing? Stir-fry.

A single Chinese word, *chao,* summarizes the two actions for which we need two English words: the action of the cook—*stir*—and the action of the oil on the food—*fry*—are contained in the one Chinese term.

But even this expansive Chinese word leads to embellishments of gesture. Infectious, personalized rhythms come along with stir-frying because it is a *way* of cooking. Economy of fuel, food, and time; beautiful, natural ingredients that are not overcooked; optimum nutrition and taste—these are the oft-touted benefits of stir-fry. In other words, total efficiency of food and cook, and this efficiency drums a beat of energy as the cook moves through the motions. You too can stir-fry exuberantly; you can dance.

On page 4 is a generic recipe for a stir-fry. Look at the recipe. The left-hand column consolidates the steps for you. Notice that the recipe divides into two clear acts with an intermission. The stir-fry should arrange itself in your mind like this:

Cut
***

Stir-fry
Combine-fry

The heart of the recipe—actual cooking time—occurs in the stir-fry and combine-fry steps. The time elapsed may be as little as five minutes, but it can be done with ease if you organize yourself.

Generic Recipe for Stir-Fry

✳ *For all that has been said, stir-frying has its procedures and rules. The techniques and the order of steps rarely change. Thus, acquaint yourself with this generic recipe, which outlines the overall procedure.*

SERVES *(an approximation is given, although this will vary greatly, depending on whether you serve the dish as an appetizer, a small course, or a main dish; also, the serving number will depend partly on what accompanying dishes are served)*

---

1 **WASH**
vegetable

Instructions as to how to trim and wash the vegetable.

---

2 **CUT AND SEASON**
meat
various seasonings

Instructions as to cutting with or across the grain to achieve uniform pieces; very often the size of the meat pieces will match those of the vegetable. Organize all cut items on the serving platter. Also given here are instructions for seasoning the meat. Add the seasoning just before you start to heat oil. Note that these seasonings are not a marinade; you have done the real work with your knife to assure tenderness.

---

3 **STIR-FRY**
oil
flavoring, such as
garlic or shallot

The oil is added to a dry, hot wok and allowed to heat to almost smoking. Each ingredient is fried separately. Toss as for a salad, with speed indicated (leisurely, moderately, vigorously). A vegetable is sometimes covered and boiled for a few minutes. Scoop out immediately, and if followed by another wok technique, wipe or rinse the wok before adding more oil. If stir-frying a meat, usually a piece of garlic and/or shallot may be rendered in the hot oil by sizzling it until it turns brown around the edges. Then it is removed and discarded.

---

4 **COMBINE-FRY**

Add the ingredients previously stir-fried and toss to combine. Flavors and juices fuse and the entire dish reheats in a few seconds. At this point, for certain dishes, you also prepare the gravy.

---

5 **SERVE**

"Immediately" is most frequently indicated here. Garnishing or presentation suggestion often given as well as possible serving suggestion.

RUBBER ARMS AND COMPACT SPACE

Think of the short-order cook presiding over the breakfast griddle. Batter, bacon, eggs, warmed plates, and butter are within arm's reach. You also should have everything within arm's reach, or within a step away. The already cut-up ingredients can be stacked on a serving platter. The bottles of seasonings should be arranged right next to the stove. You need oil, soy sauce, sherry, salt, at the very least. Also nearby should be an empty sink, a kettle of water, and some kitchen towels.

HEAT

Maximum and responsive heat is crucial for stir-frying. A gas stove is ideal because the flames bend around the curved bowl of the wok. The flame intensity may be adjusted instantaneously. Electric burners present more problems. The heat should be set on the highest setting in most cases and when turning down the heat is called for, you instead have to pull the wok slightly off the element to wait for it to reach the lower temperature.

CUTTING

While stir-frying is the heart of a recipe, the brains are in the wielding of the knife. Cut your ingredients lovingly and carefully. No matter how well you stir-fry, your dish will only be as good as you cut the ingredients. If not uniform and small, you lose the beautiful efficiency, the taste, and the tenderness of a stir-fry.

The Chinese are fond of saying that as an apprentice, you spend three years with the knife before you ever approach the stove. If you master the cutting techniques for stir-frying, you will be able to tackle the preparations for any manner of cooking. Look again at the generic recipe. The first half involves the cutting. You can pause— for a minute or several hours—after all the ingredients are cut. It is the intermission. Take a swig of beer, get dressed for company, put the baby to bed, or run an errand. When you come back, you'll dance through your stir-fry because the hard work has already been done. It will feel like tossing a salad.

The instructions for cutting tell you to cut everything uniformly. The overall texture of a stir-fry dish must be even. Thick, chewy hunks of beef settled on the bottom crushing rounds of onions and topped by a tangle of bean sprouts is not a stir-fried dish. In this example, the smallest denominator is the bean sprouts. Everything else—beef and onions—must be cut to that size. The ingredients will naturally disperse themselves evenly and you will have a light-textured dish. The balance and contrast of beef, onion, and bean sprouts will be in every spoonful. The recipes indicate whether you should cut with or against the grain, another important facet of stir-frying.

Cutting with the grain: To cut with the grain, hold the knife parallel to the grain of the meat. This results in juicy pieces of meat.

Cutting across the grain: When cutting across the grain, hold the knife perpendicular to the grain of the meat. This results in tenderness.

Cutting on the diagonal: Hold the knife angled to the strip of food. The knife (if you are right-handed; otherwise reverse these instructions) will point at 10 o'clock while the food is at 3 o'clock. This maximizes surface area for cooking. A carrot sliced straight across would make ½- to 1-inch rounds; cut on the diagonal, it will yield long ovals of 2 inches in width across the wider part.

Cutting with a tilted knife: To cut with a tilted knife, slant the top of the blade horizontally. This also exposes more surface and gives bigger, more tender slices. The diagonal and tilted cuts can be used as you near the end of a piece of food which narrows. This way your last pieces are the same size as the first.

Slivering: First slice the meat or vegetables, then stack up and cut to matchstick size.

Dicing: First cut meat or vegetable into strips, then cut through several strips at one time.

Cutting through bone: To cut chicken through the bone, you must have a heavy Chinese cleaver with a sharp edge. The object is not to crush the bone but to cut cleanly through it. Separate the chicken into its regular five sections: two breast halves, two thighs and legs, and one back. You can discard the back if you wish. Cut through the bone at 1- to 1½-inch intervals on all the pieces by snapping your wrist and letting the cleaver fall. The weight of the knife and the sharp edge should take it clean through. Re-form the chicken pieces on the serving platter for a more formal service. If the chicken is uncooked, keep the leg pieces separate from the breast meat; stir-fry the thick, dark meat first, then add the white meat.

OIL FLAVORINGS

Prepare your garlic, shallots, and ginger for rendering after you have cut your meat and vegetables. Hold the knife blade over them and press with the head of your hand. The herbs will crush slightly. The garlic and shallot will peel easily then. Ginger is usually sliced on the diagonal about ⅛ inch thick, cut from the fresh root. A slice about the size of a teaspoon is assumed when measurements are given.

ORGANIZATION

As soon as you cut up your ingredients, you can be organizing them for the stir-fry and service. Use the platter you will serve on to hold the elements of the stir-fry. You could place the cut meat (in a small bowl) on one section of the platter, stack the colander of washed vegetables on another; the crushed garlic and ginger can rest on the edge. Often you can divide your platter into as many areas as you have items to separate. This method avoids clutter, and you can move straight from the wok to the serving platter to the table in one direct sweep.

OIL

The oil must be extremely hot and close to smoking before you begin to stir-fry. You want to sear the juices in, not boil them out. This sequence should be an automatic part of your procedure:

1. *Heat the empty and dry wok*
2. *Add the oil*
3. *Let oil get as hot as possible without smoking*
4. *Add the food*

INSTANT MEASUREMENT

Those short-order breakfast cooks never measure what they sling onto the griddle. There's no time. The efficiency of stir-frying also requires a less-than-slavish devotion to measurements. Besides, the shaking and thrusting of sauce bottles is part of the dance.

The wok and its spatula are all you need to measure. My spatula holds 1½ tablespoons liquid. Salt on one corner of it is ¼ teaspoon. A pool of oil 4 inches in diameter is 3 tablespoons. A mass of slivered beef weighing 8 ounces needs to be balanced by the same volume in slivered green peppers—about 2 cups. That's all you need. Trust your eye, and leap.

You will get confident to the point that you will not use measuring cups. Taste as you cook. Adjust to your preference. You soon will dance.

TOSS AND TURN-FRY

If I could re-coin the term, I would use "toss-and-turn fry." You toss in a big salad bowl. So you would in a wok. The curved sides of a spacious wok chase pieces of food round with speed and efficiency. At other times, you simply give the food a few turns with the spatula—a motion like folding batter or dough.

In the right-hand column, *toss* or *turn* are indicated. So are the speeds: leisurely, moderately, steadily, and vigorously. Occasionally there will be a frenetically. Sometimes, a fling-and-mop motion is called for. Use the spatula to press the meat against the wok wall, while you draw circles with your arm as if mopping; thus flinging separates the pieces.

Ingredients go into the wok all together, and come out the same way. What you toss and stir in the wok is a mixture, rather than pieces of separate elements. That is why everything is cut small and evenly, and why they cook so quickly. Pour in a colanderful of broccoli all at once; don't drop it in piece by piece. Do not overcook the ingredients, and never leave what you've done to cook in the wok. Care passionately about the extra seconds that might cause your stir-fry to dry out or overcook. This is why the instructions always indicate "scoop out." The spatula will help you shovel the elements out of the wok—both the pieces of food and the resulting gravy—with two or three quick swoops.

CLEANING WHILE COOKING

The short-order cook constantly scrapes and wipes the griddle between orders. A new ingredient means a new scene, so the old props must be cleared. So it is with wok cooking too. You must start with a clean wok for each step of a stir-fry dish. Be prepared with damp paper towels or a sponge, a kettle of cold water, and a cleared sink.

If you've just stir-fried some vegetable, scoop it out with as much of the liquid as possible. Quickly sop up the remainder with a damp towel. Add oil, and you are ready to move to the next step without turning off the heat. If you've just stir-fried some meat or just completed the final combine-fry, splash water from the kettle to cool the wok and prevent burning—it makes washing up later much easier. To go on with another stir-fry, step to the sink, rinse the wok, then quickly swipe it dry with a dry towel. Any time you see the words "scoop out" in the recipe and another wok step follows, you must clean the wok.

SAUCE VS. GRAVY

A final optional step, "gravying," may occur at the end of a stir-fry recipe. What you make at this point is what is commonly called sauce in restaurants and cookbooks. I prefer the term *gravy* because a sauce usually implies a liquid that is made separately from the food. In a stir-fry, oftentimes a starchy solution is poured into the stir-fried ingredients, binding together the liquids in the wok. I prefer to skip this step unless a liquid is organically necessary for the dish—for instance, a lo-mein dish. In these, a gravy or sauce serves as the base for the noodles, which absorb the liquid.

Beautiful, fresh ingredients—well cut and in balance with one another—do not need this shiny, starchy coating. The juices of the meat, vegetables, and seasonings form a natural liquid. Soy sauce and the moisture from wilted vegetables normally release the juices from the meat and these, with the oil used to stir-fry, form a natural gravy with a slight body. Restaurants use this thickening step because it creates a finished, shiny glaze, and often use it to dress up a somewhat ill-conceived collection of ingredients. I find these sauces thick and often heavy; the starch binds in the oil and coats the food inescapably. In ordinary home cooking, with honest ingredients, the light, natural juices of the dish are as good on rice or sopped with bread and they do not leave the heavy, clingy feeling on your tongue.

THE INGREDIENTS OF STIR-FRY

Most of my stir-fry combinations are one vegetable and one meat. This, and perhaps the stir-frying of a single leafy vegetable, is the classic use of the wok and of stir-fry. I feel that once you go beyond two items, the real finesse of stir-fry is lost. If you have fresh ingredients, you will not wish to complicate the dish any further. More is not better.

Creative combinations and complex dishes in China came from traditional recipes or were left to high ranking restaurant chefs. In my mother's and our friends' homes, one vegetable or a combination of one meat and one vegetable was the norm. Free-form combinations were rarely attempted because the given combinations were delicious and difficult to surpass. Besides, so many choices existed with everyday ingredients that the possible combinations were infinite.

Unfortunately, in America, certain restaurants have given the wrong impression of Chinese food. Multi-ingredient dishes are listed on menus as an enticement. Often, the extra bamboo shoots and water chestnuts are used to fill and stretch a dish. Because they are canned, they are inexpensive and labor free, thus thrown into too many dishes, and taste like nothing. In fact, fresh water chestnuts and bamboo shoots in season are so delectable, they invite the most austere, classic treatments. Keep your stir-fries simple, with combinations that work well. Here is a list of possible combinations, using common meats and vegetables.

With beef or lamb: asparagus, broccoli, celery, leeks, onions, peas, snow peas, and sweet peppers.

With pork: the above vegetables, plus bean sprouts, bok choy cabbage, cauliflower, chayote, green beans, jerusalem artichokes, mushrooms, napa cabbage, spinach, swiss chard.

With chicken or fish: although chicken and fish will combine very well with the vegetables listed for pork and can be stir-fried as beef and pork are, they are often subject to a silkening process before they are combined with a vegetable. Then a glaze is stirred into the dish. This fancier technique dresses up these meats which are very tender—the fish is especially delicate—so standard stir-fry procedures do not work precisely as given in the generic recipe.

Root vegetables other than onions are rarely used in stir-fries. Most roots are tasty when eaten either raw or well cooked, thus they are better suited to salads or stews. That is why turnips, radishes, and carrots are not listed. Carrots may be used sparingly for color but too much would give the stir-fry a raw taste that does not belong, while if well cooked, would give it a soft texture also out of character with stir-fries.

SAMPLE RECIPES

Here are two everyday stir-fry dishes, offered as examples and lessons of stir-fry. In these recipes, try not to use measuring cups and spoons, but feel comfortable using the spatula to approximate the quantities you need. Further, you may soon wish to try your own combinations from the preceding list. Once you feel comfortable with stir-fry, other wok recipes and techniques fall into place.

Beef and Celery

 Celery has enough character to combine with pork and beef.

SERVES 2 AS A MAIN COURSE WITH RICE, 4 AS A SMALL COURSE

1 **TRIM AND CUT**
6 stalks celery

Use the stalks at the heart if possible. String the stalks of celery. Cut each with a tilted knife blade into slices ⅛ to ¼ inch thick.

2 **CUT AND SEASON**
8 ounces boneless beef, preferably flank steak
1 tablespoon soy sauce
1 tablespoon sherry

Cut meat into slices similar in thickness and size to the celery. Mix with soy sauce and sherry in a bowl.

3 **STIR-FRY**
1 tablespoon oil
salt

Heat 1 tablespoon oil in wok set over high heat. When oil is hot, add celery and stir-fry at a leisurely pace until translucent tender, about 30 seconds. Salt lightly. Scoop out while still crisp. Wipe wok.

4 **STIR-FRY**
2 tablespoons oil
1 clove garlic

Heat oil and add garlic; render until it turns a little brown at edges, then discard. Add meat and stir-fry vigorously for about 30 seconds.

5 **COMBINE-FRY**

When meat is no longer pink, add the celery and toss to combine and reheat.

6 **SERVE**

Serve immediately with plain rice.

Grand Wok Cookbook

Artichokes and Mayonnaise
in a Waterlily Setting

PAGE 47

Pork and Cauliflower

An infallible combination. The cauliflower, if covered and slightly boiled in the wok after stir-frying, absorbs the juices and seasonings of the pork. In this recipe, I give an example of a stir-fry for which a gravy is made at the end.

SERVES 2 AS A MAIN COURSE, 4 AS A SMALL COURSE

---

1 **WASH AND TRIM**
1 head cauliflower

Rinse the cauliflower and trim flowerets to a uniform height of 1 inch. Slice lengthwise where necessary so flowerets are no thicker than ¼ inch. You should have about 3 cups of flowerets.

---

2 **CUT AND SEASON**
8 ounces boneless pork
2 tablespoons soy sauce, preferably light
1 tablespoon sherry
1 teaspoon cornstarch

Peel or cut off extraneous membranes. Cut meat into ⅛- to ¼-inch slices across the grain. Place in a bowl and, just before stir-frying, pour in soy sauce, sherry, and cornstarch. Mix well.

---

3 **STIR-FRY**
1½ tablespoons oil
salt
½ to ¾ cup water

Heat wok, then add 1½ tablespoons oil. Allow oil to get hot, then add the cauliflower and toss. When the pieces are thoroughly heated, add the water. Salt lightly, and cover to let vegetable boil until tender, about 3 minutes. It will appear opaque, however do not let it become soft. Scoop out cauliflower and any liquid left in wok. Wipe wok with a dry towel.

---

4 **STIR-FRY**
2 tablespoons oil
1 clove garlic, lightly crushed

Heat wok and add 2 tablespoons oil. Render garlic until brown around edges, then remove and discard. Add the pork and stir-fry until meat turns color, about 1 minute.

---

5 **COMBINE-FRY**
2 tablespoons cornstarch mixed with 2 tablespoons water

When pork is white, add the cauliflower. Stir moderately to combine and reheat. Bring juices in wok to a boil. While stirring with the inverted spatula, pour in most of the cornstarch paste. Continue stirring until the juices have thickened, and come to a boil again. The gravy will turn shiny and opaque. If not thick enough for your taste, add remainder of the paste and stir until thickened.

---

6 **SERVE**

Serve immediately with rice.

FINAL WORDS

When all is said and done, it is useful to remember what a stir-fry is **not:**

It is not a chop-suey of every ingredient under the sun. Balance and complementary flavors ought to be considered. Refer to the suggested combinations (page 9).

It is not a barely heated salad. Vegetables should not be raw. A stir-fried vegetable is thoroughly heated, and it retains a degree of natural resiliency, still plump and crunchy, but it is cooked.

It is not a random collection of sizes and shapes. Everything must be cut to one size and shape to cook evenly and quickly, and remain tender.

It is not an open invitation to throw in a can of bamboo shoots or water chestnuts.

It is not food you leave in the pan until you are ready to serve. Scoop out what you've stir-fried. The beauty and efficiency of stir-fry is lost if food is kept hot in the pan—it will overcook.

It is not difficult to learn stir-fry.

It is not something to try for the first time if you aren't prepared to scrub your stovetop afterwards.

It is not an instant cure for obesity, although it can help.

It is not the only way I ever cook.

Other Techniques for the Wok

The wok is excellent for steaming, deep-frying, and braising. Let's take a look at each.

STEAMING

The most subtle way of cooking in a wok is steaming. It is a method less well known than stir-frying, but it is the basis of a wonderful repertory of simple, natural, clean, and—often—quick cuisine.

This is not steam under pressure, as in a pressure cooker, but rather the natural vapor of water cooking. And not just vegetables are steamed, but red meat, chicken, fish, custards, and desserts. Imagine the extent of moisture retention in these items without the hot, drying air of an oven. Since this is steam cooking without pressure, foods are not cooked until lifeless or tenderized beyond recognition. And contrary to some Western expectations of rather bland steamed food, wok-steamed dishes are well seasoned. Meats and fish come out in a pool of their own juices blended with seasonings and wine, making a simple gravy. It is a naturally good way of cooking, becoming ever more popular. French chefs, for example, are cooking more and more *à la vapeur,* as they search for means of gently cooking vegetables.

Most woks come equipped with a domed, roomy lid and a steaming rack. The lid allows the steam to swirl above the dish, which sits on the rack over boiling water. Bring about 2 inches of water to a boil in the wok with the rack in place. Then place the food in a steaming dish and place the dish on the rack. Cover wok with the lid, and the steaming begins. When a recipe requires lengthy steaming, tiered bamboo steamers are preferable because you can easily add additional water to the bottom of the wok. To steam successfully, keep the following points in mind:

Food steamed in a wok must go in a plate. In very rare instances, the food may be placed directly on the rack (in which case, I prefer a rack of natural woven bamboo, rattan, or reed; see Equipment).

The plate must be shallow. The shape and size of the plate is crucial. It must be shallow so the food is exposed evenly to the steam above, and it must be deep enough to catch the juices. Choose a plate that allows a 1-inch clearance between it and the wok at the plate's circumference, so that the steam can rise around the plate to swirl under the cover. Whatever dish you plan to use, test it in the wok on the rack to make sure the steam will billow around and above it, and make sure the lid will fit with a tight seal. (See Equipment for more about steaming plates.)

Steam in the serving dish. It is advisable to steam in the dish in which you plan to serve. As a rule, steaming will not hurt fine china, since it does not get hotter than the temperature of steam itself. The food stays hot, and no juices are lost. You may also lift the dish out of the wok and place it into or onto a larger, attractive cold serving platter. This second platter serves also to decorate and frame the original plate. Moreover, you won't have to bring a very hot and slightly wet dish to the table.

Arrange the food in a single layer. It is important that the food be in a single layer so that steam touches its surface evenly.

Check and refill the water in the wok as you steam. Add additional boiling water to the wok when the level of the water sinks too low. Keep a kettle of simmering water on hand for very long steaming. Two inches of water kept at a high boil will be evaporated within 15 to 20 minutes, depending on the size of your wok. Most foods which you steam will take less than that amount of time.

Use hot pads to lift the dish out of the steamer. Wear padded hot gloves if possible, when removing dishes from the steamer; or buy and use a plate lifter, available in oriental hardware stores. It is easy to get burned.

Use the following recipe to practice your steaming technique.

Zucchini Knuckles

In this recipe, cross sections of zucchini are seeded, then refilled with a mixture of pork and cured black beans, resembling bone and marrow. It is a dish of simple, elegant tastes. No additional fat or starch is needed—the juices of the meat and vegetable intermingle for a light, natural liquid that is wonderful spooned over rice.

SERVES 2 AS A MAIN COURSE, 4 AS A SMALL COURSE

1	**SOAK** 1 tablespoon salted black beans	Rinse beans, then soak in a bowl of cold water while you prepare the squash.
2	**PEEL AND CUT** 1 pound small zucchini, no longer than 8 inches	Peel zucchini if they are not young. Cut zucchini into 1½-inch sections. Hollow out the seeded sections. Going around the outside of the squash, punch the tines of a fork through into the hollow in 3 or 4 places.
3	**MIX** ½ to ¾ pound boneless pork, such as Boston butt, ground if desired 1 teaspoon sherry 1 clove garlic 1 teaspoon light soy sauce	Mince the meat if you haven't bought it already ground. Place meat in a bowl. Drain and then coarsely chop the black beans, and add to the meat. Add the seasonings and mix well.
4	**STUFF**	Fill the prepared zucchini with the meat mixture, then arrange the zucchini on a steaming plate, standing upright with the filling showing.
5	**STEAM**	Bring water to a boil in a wok, with rack in place. Place plate of squash on rack, cover wok, and steam over medium-high heat for 15 to 20 minutes, or until the pork is cooked. Insert a fork into the meat. If the juices run clear, it is done.
6	**SERVE**	Serve immediately with rice.

The demi-sphere of the wok is ideal for deep-frying. Economical and efficient, the wok allows you to get a depth of oil in the center but also have room for maneuvering. Six cups of oil in a wok will fry a whole chicken or duck in a sea of oil, but 6 cups in a normal straight-sided pot is a mere wading pool.

Fried foods have unjustly gained a bad reputation for being greasy and fattening. With the right technique, good oil and a deep-fry thermometer, your food will come out aromatic and piping hot without greasiness. Deep-fried food is rich, but no richer than any dish with a sauce containing butter and flour. If the oil is fresh and hot enough, only a minimal amount is absorbed. Spring rolls, for example, are crisp and light primarily because just the right amount of oil is taken in to separate the layers of rolled pastry and make them flaky. In other instances, the deep-frying goes just deep enough to seal in the essence of the food.

In the tradition of Chinese wok cooking, I present an entire repertory of foods that are cooked in deep oil without batter. These are worth discovering—French-fried Vegetables and Glazed Soft-shelled Crabs are some examples.

To deep-fry, keep the following in mind:

Have your oil hot enough. It is helpful to use a deep-frying thermometer. The oil must be hot enough before any food can be inserted, and 350 to 370 degrees is the normal temperature range for deep-frying. However, certain recipes take a lower setting, and normally are those foods which are not browned but rather sealed. If you don't have a thermometer, watch for the oil to become less viscous. As it gets hotter, the currents in the oil agitate it faster. Insert a wooden chopstick or spoon so that it touches the bottom of the wok. If a string of bubbles stream up, the oil is ready. Or throw in a piece of bread or a sprinkling of flour; if they float and sizzle immediately, the oil is ready.

Avoid splattering the oil. If you toss the food into the hot oil, it is likely to splatter. Ease items into the oil carefully. In particular, very big pieces of food—whole chicken or pork cutlets—may be lowered into the boiling oil without fear by easing them down the side of the wok, surrendering them to the curled walls. Nothing needs to dive and splash into mid-wok.

Fry small amounts of food at one time. Once the oil is ready, fry only conservative amounts of food at once. This prevents the oil from cooling too radically or putting too much moisture into the oil. The recipe for Roasted Shrimp works because the shrimp are never allowed to stay in the oil for very long.

Use the correct tool to retrieve food. I advise using chopsticks or tongs to handle large pieces of food. A fork will pierce food, destroying the protective coating and letting juices escape while splattering and exploding in the oil. The perforated ladle is crucial for smaller pieces.

Try your deep-frying technique on the following recipe.

Breaded Pork Cutlets

 Such a premium is placed on veal that pork is quite overlooked. Really fine veal is all but unavailable, but superb pork is accessible. This is a starkly simple recipe, easy to do in a wok. I leave the bone in; it seems to preserve the meat juices better. You may find as I do, that these are preferable to chicken or veal.

SERVES 4 AS A MAIN COURSE

1 **SEASON**
4 center loin pork chops—from ⅜ to 1 inch thick
salt and pepper to taste

Sprinkle salt and pepper on both sides of the chops. Prick the meat with a fork to allow the seasoning to penetrate.

2 **HEAT**
4 cups oil

This is more oil than you may be used to, but with this method, both sides of the chops are heated at the same time. Pour oil into wok and bring to 350 degrees.

3 **COAT**
1 egg
2 cups fresh bread crumbs

Beat the egg. Place bread crumbs on a sheet of waxed paper. Both the egg and crumbs should be close to the stove. When the oil is hot, begin to bread the chops.

4 **DEEP-FRY**

One by one, immerse the chop in the egg and immediately turn onto the bread crumbs. Then flip over to do the other side with crumbs. Repeat with second chop. Slide chops into the wok and deep-fry. They will be almost submerged in oil. Turn when the bottom surfaces are a deep golden brown, and cook second side until they turn the same color. Do the same for remaining chops; a ⅜-inch chop should take 7 to 10 minutes to deep-fry. Remove chops and check by cutting near the bone to make certain it is done.

5 **SERVE**

Serve plain, perhaps with some Worcestershire sauce.

I turn to braising, or stewing, for everyday cooking; it makes a heartier and more fulfilling meal than a stir-fry, especially in cold weather. And a stew that is a family favorite welcomes company better than many a fancier dish.

The wok is ideal for braising because so often a dish requires that onions first be sauteed in oil, then the meat be browned too. All this can be done in the wok very easily. In the case of chicken and fish, braising is really just a stir-frying with liquid added at the end; then the mixture is covered to braise for only 15 or 20 minutes. A beef stroganoff or goulash, if made with a tender cut of meat, is merely a variation on a stir-fry with a short braising at the end. And curries are my favorite short "stew" to cook in a wok.

Note, however, that braising in a wok will occasionally break down the seasoned surface, particularly if the sauce is acidic. If you use a wok very frequently, I suggest having 2 woks—one for stir-frying and deep-frying and one for braising, steaming, and poaching.

There are a few special points to remember when braising in a wok:

Check amount of liquid. Since liquid evaporates faster in a wok than in a straight-sided pot, you must check more often and replenish the stewing gravy with stock, water, or wine. I often start the stew in the wok and transfer it to a heavy pot for unsupervised slow cooking.

Reducing takes less time. Once a stew is cooked and you wish to reduce the liquid and concentrate the sauce, you'll find that the time it takes to boil down is less than a standard pot. More surface is exposed in a wok and it is only a matter of minutes after you turn up the heat and lift off the lid that the gravy thickens and concentrates.

Try your skill at braising, this time in a wok.

Lamb Braised with White Radish

 This is a hearty, peasant stew. The robust taste and aroma of dark soy sauce mixes well with the flavor of the lamb, and the biting juiciness of the radish modifies to a unique sweetness. It takes only one step of stir-frying—10 minutes of active cooking—then you forget about it while it cooks ever so slowly.

SERVES 4 TO 6 AS A MAIN COURSE

1

CUT
2 pounds boneless lamb, shoulder or leg
3 scallions
2 slices gingerroot

Cut meat into 1-inch cubes. Cut roots off the scallions and cut each scallion in half. Set ginger out.

2

STIR-FRY
2 tablespoons oil

Heat oil in wok over high heat and then add the ginger and scallions. When the scallions are wilted, add the meat and stir-fry until cooked on the outside—about 8 minutes.

3

SEASON AND BRAISE
3 tablespoons dark soy sauce
1 tablespoon light soy sauce
2 tablespoons sherry
2 teaspoons sugar
1 star anise
1 teaspoon Sichuan peppercorns

When the meat is no longer red on the outside add the seasonings to the wok. Let the liquids bubble, then add water to cover along with the spices. Cover and bring to a boil. Turn heat down so the mixture just simmers and let cook for 3 to 4 hours. Check liquid in about 1½ hours and if braising liquid is more than half-way down, add more water.

4

ADD
2 cups peeled and diced white radish (daikon)

One hour before serving, add the radish and bring stew to a boil again, making sure the radish pieces are covered with liquid. Add more water if necessary. Cover again and continue to cook until radish is tender, about 45 minutes.

5

REDUCE

When the radish is tender, turn up the heat and lift off the lid. Cook liquid at a boil until it is reduced to about 1 cup. Ladle meat and radish into a serving dish. Pour gravy over meat through a strainer, catching the herbs. Discard herbs and serve stew with rice and dark beer.

OTHER USES FOR THE WOK

You can poach fish, fry hamburgers and steaks, make omelettes, and roast herbs in a wok. You will find that even cooking hamburgers in a wok is easy because the curved sides help you flip them over. The cook at my parents' home made a kind of crêpe which she filled and rolled right in the wok! Once you become adept at using this pan and learn to live with it, you will find it a utilitarian and friendly cooking companion.

A Note on Equipment

A wok is a work-horse—a universal cooking pan. So many varied culinary techniques take place in the wok that it must be durable and strong. Own a good-sized wok. Don't be intimidated by the looks of a 14- or 16-inch wok. You don't ever fill it. You don't ever even half-fill it. For stir-frying, a ⅓-filled wok maximizes heat use and tossing space. Remember, the wok functions like a salad bowl; you couldn't toss in a salad bowl that is filled to the rim.

Woks come in varied shapes. Some are more flared while others more rounded. I find the deeper ones useful for all-around purposes, although the flatter ones are easier for handling big pieces of food or making an omelette. If you cook on an electric stove, find a wok with a flat bottom. It will be more stable on the element although it is also well-suited to a gas stove.

A wok should be made of a good heat-retaining metal. Carbon-steel woks are common in this country, and they retain heat and season well. A heavy, copper-bottomed stainless-steel wok, however, has the advantage of being easy to clean; unfortunately, if hot oil is kept a fraction of a second too long in a stainless-steel wok, unsightly burn marks will coat parts of the surface, and they are then difficult to remove. Although not suitable for stir-frying, a stainless-steel wok is good for steaming and braising. You don't have to worry about re-oiling it afterwards. Carbon-steel woks tend to rust if not dried immediately after washing, and, once in a while—with 30 seconds over a hot burner—they need to be lightly oiled after steaming. The best choice is a combination of both: one wok (carbon-steel) for fat frying; one (stainless-steel) for water cooking.

Woks with nonstick surfaces, such as Silverstone, would seem to be a breeze to work in if they didn't peel or scratch. Some very tough cooking over extremely high heat goes on in a wok, and it is no place for a delicate surface. The woks made of anodized metals are supreme, although expensive and not widely known.

Electric woks are a clever idea but they have limitations. They cannot be taken off the heat source, so you must move fast to remove the ingredients from the wok. Cleaning the wok between steps of stir-fried dishes also presents a problem. But if a cook is comfortable and practiced with the wok spatula-shovel, the food can be removed very quickly, and so can residual oil and juices.

Wooden handles are helpful. Most wok cooking will be done on the highest heat setting, and the handles—whether single or double—get very hot. Although the wooden handles are prone to some scorching—either from the heat beneath or the burner to its side—you can save yourself the frantic search for potholders each time you wish to move the wok (which is frequent on an electric stove).

THE SPATULA-SHOVEL

This is the essential companion to the wok. You can do things with a spatula which can take the place of a spoon, a scraper, a strainer, and a knife. The rounded tip of the spatula and the curve of the wok let you scoop things out, including liquid, with just swoops of the arm. You don't have to lift the wok to retrieve all but a few drops of liquid. If you need to drain the food while spooning it out, just hold the spatula of food against the wall of the wok, tipping it so the liquid runs back out. And of course, you can use the spatula to measure while you cook.

THE LID

This dome-shaped cover is crucial, and the roomier it is the better. When steam is trapped under it, the lid allows the steam to flow efficiently around and billow over the food. Make sure you get a lid that fits with a good seal. Little steam should seep out while steaming or braising.

THE WIRE SCOOP AND PERFORATED LADLE

Used to gather pieces out of deep-fat, these are strainers that can mobilize a great deal of food in one scoop.

THE LADLE

This spoon is angled to dip and scoop large amounts of liquid in the wok.

THE STEAMING RACK

The steaming rack separates the water from the dish holding the food. Most wok sets are sold with a metal or natural rack. The latter is often a bare criss-cross of sticks. I prefer the circular perforated trays, especially the bamboo or rattan ones. I also have several extras on hand for stacking when I steam large quantities of little pastries or vegetables in continuous batches. Bamboo also gives just a hint of its nutty, piney, fragrance, which is attractive in pastries and vegetables. Although totally flat disks of bamboo or rattan are difficult to find in this country, one can improvise a few by using the flattest round baskets or trays sold on the market. The three-tiered bamboo stacking steamers impart a fragrance to steamed foods too, and these are made to stack in the wok. All of these woven natural racks age and season beautifully with use, taking on an increasingly darker color; furthermore, the steam and water can breathe through the weave of the natural material.

STEAMING DISHES

You can substitute a variety of dishes for preparing the steamed foods in this book. Shallow baking dishes and glass and ceramic pie plates sometimes work, although they are often too big to fit beneath the lid of the wok. Soup plates which flare out may also be used, as can Italian pasta plates. Ideal, of course, are Chinese serving plates which are largely flat, but slope down ever so gently from the sides. They hold the gravies and juices well, and there are no seams or sharp angles; they are the perfect compromise of bowl and plate. With two or three such steaming plates, you will be able to cook every steamed dish in this book, from a whole salmon to a cheesecake.

MORTAR AND PESTLE

In Asian cookery, the most common mortar and pestle is made of heavy granite. Rather than crushing and grinding, the ingredients are pounded into a paste. The pestle is lifted about 8 inches from the mortar and ceaselessly thumped over the ingredients. Not only spices are worked over in the mortar, but also onions, vegetables, shrimp, and meat. The Thai curry paste typifies this use of the mortar and pestle. Luckily, we have blenders and food processors to do the work for us, though the results are not exactly the same. Small quantities, hard seeds, and garlic are pulverized into a smooth paste in the mortar and pestle; the machines just do not do the same job but do come close. The mortar and pestle is an extremely useful kitchen apparatus and distinctive, too. I constantly use mine.

KNIFE

You must have a good knife—and the equipment to keep it sharp. Cutting spells the success or failure of stir-frying, and it is worth going to any length to own at least one good knife. A Chinese cleaver is very versatile, and, contrary to its large and heavy appearance, does fine work beautifully. Its squared corners and straight sides help you to cut and eye the geometric shapes clearly. There is no need to roll the knife since the edge is a straight line, and therefore you need not waste motion or time. But the ethnic origins of your knife are not so important as simply having a good one and using it well.

MEASURING UTENSILS

As mentioned earlier, the spirit and tradition of stir-fry does not really accommodate the slow, separate tools of measurement you might be used to. I have made some recommendations already, which use the tools of cooking to measure. Here they are:

> *a spatula-shovelful = 1½ to 2 tablespoons*
> *a corner of the spatula-shovel = ¼ teaspoon*
> *a 4-inch pool in the wok = 3 tablespoons*
> *5 spews from the soy sauce bottle = ½ teaspoon*

Verify these measurements with your own equipment—they might differ slightly depending on the type and brand you own. Once you know them, liberate yourself from spoons and cups and enjoy the ease of wok cooking.

Just as you would shake or pinch salt and pepper, spoon mustard, pour ketchup, or shake hot sauce, you can learn to judge the amounts of these basic ingredients for a stir-fry: soy sauce, oil, salt and pepper, red chili pepper, sherry, and Madeira. Many brands of soy sauce come with a sealed plastic stopper; you cut the raised plastic part to open a hole from which you can pour. The recipes which are not marked with a footnote are ones in which I hope you will follow without strict measurements. Those marked with notes are ones for which exact proportions are crucial. Likewise, if you feel you cannot at all imagine the final result of a recipe, then cook your first attempt using the standard measurement.

OTHER ACCESSORIES

The following pieces of equipment are companions helpful to wok cookery. You should have them conveniently placed.

wine spouts (for certain soy sauces, sherry, Madeira)

oil can, or container with a small opening

water kettle

brown kitchen towels (matches soy sauce)

lazy susan with seasonings on it

pair of hot-pad mittens

bowls to hold salt and/or oil

Ingredients

My aim throughout this book has been to use mainly foods that are on the shelves of local supermarkets. It has been encouraging in the last ten years to see items once thought eclectic, or at least ethnic, make inroads into large grocery stores. It is now possible to cook Chinese, Italian, Mexican, Greek, or French with a trip to just one food store—the same store you go to for milk, toilet paper, and detergent. This is all well and good, however it is the dedicated cook who tracks down the ingredients that are worthwhile. Convenience is one thing, but the chase for the elusive, or the freshest, or the best contributes to the adventure of cooking.

I encourage you to search out the nearest Asian food store. In an Asian store, you will find a wide selection of soy sauces and fish sauce, but also good and reasonably priced garlic, cooking oil, and varieties of rice. You will likely also find a better quality, thinner, and finer wonton pastry, and you'll certainly get fresher tofu. Stock up on ingredients of high quality which are basic to the foods you cook. Practically speaking, you'll get a better price and a better product than what you'll see in the supermarket gourmet sections. Moreover, many of the Chinese and Southeastern Asian items are easy to store and they last a good while—a phenomenon attributable to the extremely ancient and widespread techniques of curing and sun-drying.

I have found the easiest way to communicate with an Asian proprietor is to ask simply what days the fresh perishable ingredients are delivered. You will improve the taste of your food if you merely buy these ingredients when they are freshest. The Asian stores of most small cities and towns are supplied once a week by truck. Asians will come out in droves the day that the tofu, greens, and fresh fruits arrive. You can be one of the many who eagerly awaits the weekly delivery.

Like the recipes in this book, ingredients are often inter-culinary. That is, you may find yourself using some Asian products in what would normally be considered Western dishes. Likewise, you may want to incorporate traditional Western products in making your improvisational stir-fries. My philosophy of searching for quality ingredients doesn't stop at Asian stores; I hope you will shop selectively for olive oil, cheeses, and vinegars from neighborhood shops specializing in Italian, Greek, or French food. Many products are also available by mail order from reliable packers such as Williams-Sonoma in California.

Three basic ingredients—rice, soy sauce, and oil—are central to the recipes in this book, and they are described first. I follow this basic information with descriptions and tips on other frequently used items, from meats, poultry, and fish; to noodles and pastas; to seasonings and spices. I hope you will approach these and other foods that might be new to you with a sense of adventure and excitement. Let the wok bring you new cooking techniques, but also introduce you to the foods that were originally cooked in it.

RICE

This cookbook is not a Chinese cookbook, but I emphasize rice because it is the crucial accompaniment to many of the dishes. How could I disregard a food which is at the root of Chinese cuisine, and therefore of wok cooking?

Rice and soy sauce are a very special pair of tastes in food. The bond between them is like bread and butter or like bread and wine—one of the world's few basic and incomparable affinities. Even in Western cuisines, it is hard to find as versatile an accompaniment as rice. Compared with freshly baked bread or homemade noodles, rice has the least fat and is the least salty type of starch to serve at a meal. And rice is so very easy to store and fix.

For most recipes in this book, rice is best cooked Asian style; that is, *without salt or fat*. Stir-fried foods have strong tastes which begin with the use of soy sauce. Foods spiced with hot chili peppers are likewise intense. The best background to these foods is plain rice. It contrasts with more highly seasoned dishes, and lends a natural sweet taste that is ideal for balancing the salt or sting in the dish.

The Irish know potatoes, the French bread, and the Italian pasta. Asians know rice. Grown on native ground, Asian rice is superb. But good rice is also available in our own backyard. You will find a wide selection of domestic and imported rice at any Asian market. Short-grained rice is popular with northern Asians, while long-grain rice is used more by those in the south. The grains are good in different ways, but I find that the type of grain is less important in the flavor of rice than are its qualities of smell and taste. Of the average supermarket fare, I prefer Carolina rice for its aroma, sweetness, and texture. In any case, don't buy converted rice, which tastes musty and is mealy.

Jasmine or Basmati rice from Thailand is now available in Asian markets. The name *Jasmine* refers to its fine fragrance when cooked. This is truly a superior rice that becomes shiny and opaque as it cooks. A transparent cream cloaks each pearl-white kernel, making the rice a little sticky like the insides of a potato. Some slight clinging of the kernels is the way any rice should be served.

Glutinous rice, also called sweet rice, is a short-grain rice that is quite sticky and extremely chewy when cooked. It is the basis for many sweets and desserts. The flour milled from this rice is used to make pastries and noodles, and is featured in the recipe Sweet Rice Balls (page 211). It is available in Asian groceries.

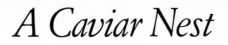

A Caviar Nest

PAGE **48**

Light Pâté with Beer and Brown Peppercorns

PAGE 50

Plain Boiled Rice

 This recipe will not fail, whether you are making ¹/₂ cup or 25 pounds of rice.

SERVES VARIABLE NUMBER OF PEOPLE

1 | **WASH**
¹/₂ to 1 cup rice per person

Pour rice into a saucepan large enough to accommodate the rice after it doubles or triples in cooking. Run water into the pot, and knead and shuffle the kernels through your fingers. Pour off the water and repeat 1 more time.

2 | **ADD**
water to cover by ³/₄ inch

Run water into the saucepan until it covers the surface of the rice. Tilt the pot to settle the rice, and then add water until level is about ³/₄ inch above the surface of the rice. (Most Asians will brush the surface of the rice with their index finger—if the water level is at the first joint, measurement is exact.) Add a little more water if you like your rice slightly softer.

3 | **COOK**

Cover saucepan and place on high heat until water boils. Immediately turn heat to low and, with cover on, cook for 15 to 20 minutes until rice is tender.

4 | **SERVE**

Serve rice with a wooden spoon, gently scraping and turning. The surface will at first look matted and dry. A few holes appear in this surface; this is where the last bits of water escape from the bottom of the pot. As you rake with the spoon, steam will swirl up; this lets off excess moisture.

NOTE: The reason this method of water measurement works is that each grain of rice absorbs only the water around it. The amount of water above the rice is relative, being consigned to evaporation in the normal boiling and heating of the water.

OIL

Oil for wok cooking is efficient and leaves no trace of itself, like a good butler. Also like a butler, it should have a high smoking point; that is, it should burn only at extreme heat and agitation. Corn oil, peanut oil, soy oil, safflower oil, and mixtures of oils are perfectly acceptable for stir-fries. Avoid those oils which are heavy and thick. If you can taste or feel them coating the food and your tongue, you should not be using them for stir-frying or deep-frying. In certain cases, however, the flavor of the oil is necessary, such as in recipes calling for olive oil, walnut oil, or sesame oil. Whereas most recipes simply say "oil," these ingredients are specified and you should use what is listed.

Don't be afraid to use oil in frying. It is crucial to good cooking. The oil lubricates and prevents sticking; it also heats to a very high temperature, smoothing textures and sealing in precious juices. There is no question that when we turn to fancier preparations, more oil is necessary, just as more and more butter is required to enrich sauces and make lighter pastries. But in an age of concern about calories and cholesterol, remember the versatility of oil. Compared with the amount of oil in a typical salad dressing, the oil in a stir-fried dish is much less. That is why 4 table-spoons of oil to stir-fry a pound of spinach or other greens is not much at all; think of how much oil you would use in the dressing of raw spinach.

SOY SAUCE

The French translate the term with more success: *essence de soja*. There's nothing about this extract of soy beans that is remotely like a sauce. *Essence* and *oil* give a much better clue to its use, as well. Soy sauce is a distinct seasoning. If good, it should be used sparingly. Like a vinegar or brandy or aged cheese, the flavor should be deep and long-lasting. Unfortunately to some people, using soy sauce means drowning the food in a deep, thick, and dark liquid. A high-quality light soy sauce (also labeled "thin soy sauce" or "superior soy sauce") hardly colors the food.

In this country, and for practical purposes, buy the imported varieties from Japan or China. The Chinese soy sauces tend to come in two types: dark and light. Light soy sauce is much more salty and the flavor more subtle. When used with light meats such as pork or chicken, it will not brown the flesh. Dark soy sauce is processed with molasses and has a robust flavor, less salty. It is used with red meats in stir-frying and in all stews because it imparts a hearty brown color. (Dark soy sauce is sometimes labeled "mushroom soy sauce" or "shrimp soy sauce" because additional flavors are added to it. These flavors are subtle and mushroom soy sauce is usable any time dark soy sauce is indicated.) Finally, there is an extremely thick and dark soy sauce, sold as "double-dark soy sauce" or "thick soy sauce." I specify double-dark only in my recipe for Chicken Rice, but it can be used in small quantities anytime dark soy is listed, especially in stews. Just a little of it will imbue the stew with a wonderfully rich and robust color.

If light and dark soy sauces are not available, use a medium soy sauce, such as Kikkoman. Tamari is an acceptable substitute, but avoid teriyaki sauce. Read the label. If it contains sugar, MSG, and other flavor boosters, avoid it. In the recipes for this book, you may substitute medium soy sauce if you don't have light or dark soy; if unspecified and you have only light and dark, use half and half.

Use soy sauce as you would salt. When you are at the final step in a stir-fry or about to slowly stew a mixture, taste it. If not salty enough, adjust to taste with soy sauce. Some brands of soy sauce come with plastic caps. Once you cut the nubs off, they become holes through which you can pour controlled quantities of soy sauce.

MEATS, POULTRY, AND FISH

Meat: In general, the younger or smaller cuts of meat are more tender and better suited for stir-frying. Choose beef that is bright red in color; pork should be pale with small, even marbling. Buy choice sections, even though they are apt to cost more. You will already be using much less to feed more people—four, six, or eight ounces of meat will serve up to four people. Flank steak and tenderloin tips of beef and pork are not so costly when figured this way. And there will be less waste—both in the meat and in your time in trimming it. These better cuts will slice easily into regular shapes because the grain is easy to read. If using steaks, choose thicker pieces; then you can stand the piece on end to cut across the grain. With the best cuts of meat and the right cutting techniques, the results will be very tender pieces, quickly tossed in oil.

Many recipes call for minced meat—either pork, veal, or beef. Although meat ground at the store is acceptable, it is much better to grind or mince your own, especially pork. Chopping by hand or in the food processor produces a much more satisfactory result: the meat is finer, more tender, and the juices held in longer. To get the most control of the chopping—by hand or by machine—make sure you cut the meat into small, thin pieces before putting it into the machine or giving it a fast chop with the cleaver. Uneven slices will yield an uneven mixture that is at once pastelike and coarse. Watch your processor, however; it can very easily spin the meat into an unpalatable paste.

Poultry: In much of East Asia, chicken costs the same as duck, sometimes more. This high price is partly a reflection of the place chicken has in the ranking of food. It is crucial to buy chicken as fresh as possible. If you can, go to a farmers market or natural foods store, where the chickens are less likely to have been adulterated by hormones or to have been packaged and transported long distances. In really delicate recipes, such as Chicken Rice or Brown Chicken, starting with a really fresh bird is critical, because the cooking methods serve to enhance the natural tastes of the chicken.

Turkey: In addition to whole turkeys, selected parts of the turkey are now found in the markets year-round. These parts include the breast (sometimes half the breast), legs, wings, and the fillet of the breast. The breast, if not too large, works well in a recipe such as Whiskeyed Turkey. The fillet of the breast is the most tender piece of white meat, couched lengthwise along either side of the breast bone ridge. It is suitable for cutting and stir-frying and, although expensive, has no waste and the grain of the flesh is clearly exposed, allowing you to cut it easily.

Fish: A fresh whole fish is much tastier than fillets. The skin retains its juices, and the bone flavors the flesh. When I say "whole fish," I mean a fish with its head on. Juices escape from a headed fish though less easily than from a fillet, so if you can, leave the head on. The fish is also more attractive when served with the head on.

When shopping for fish to cook in your wok, do not buy one weighing more than 1½ to 2 pounds. Make sure it looks lively, with shiny skin, clear eyes, and with a flesh that feels firm to the touch. If your recipe calls for fillets, have the fishmonger fillet the fish just before you buy it; the longer fillets stand out, the more they lose flavor. When buying fillets, make sure they smell sweet and are plump and resilient.

For the recipes in this book, choose flounder, sole, turbot, halibut (and all others in the flat whitefish family), pompano, grouper, sea and lake trout, snapper, salmon, and other fish with light meat. Black sea bass and grouper are also Chinese favorites, prized for their silky texture. Tuna and mackerel do not work as well.

Serve one fish per person if it is meant as a main course. Two fish can fit on a plate if each weighs 1½ pounds. If you have a stacking bamboo steamer, it is even easier to cook multiple servings. But if your single fish is meant as one dish in a selection of courses, then serve the whole fish in the communal Chinese style, with each guest reaching in to scoop up a biteful of fish.

Seafood: Mussels and oysters in the shell must be as fresh as possible and the shells closed tight. Lobsters must be fresh and very fiesty. If your fishmonger knows how to choose one, ask for a female, because then you'll be able to enjoy the coral as well. Scallops are usually sold shelled, and for most recipes in this book, the smaller bay scallops are preferable. All scallops should be moist appearing and firm. Shrimp are best when purchased whole with their heads on, although that is less common. In particular, use whole shrimp for the Whole Fried Shrimp and Braised Shrimp recipes. Shrimp is one of the few seafoods that does not suffer much when frozen, but buy frozen shrimp only in its uncooked state. Cooked frozen shrimp becomes mushy when cooked. Crabmeat is better tasting when frozen than canned, but use fresh if you can get it. Asian markets often carry crabmeat at a better price than regular stores.

VEGETABLES (INCLUDING BEAN SPROUTS AND TOFU)

A variety of vegetables are used in this book, and most are available at supermarkets, although better grades of bok choy and snow peas can be found in Asian markets. In general, vegetables should be fresh looking and tender. Choose the small but compact and heavy heads of bok choy, and select snow peas that have not yet bulged. Don't let greater size lure you into choosing big items, which are often tough and tasteless. Other vegetables and greens, such as turnip greens and spinach, should also be chosen for tenderness, not size. Once home, wash and pick through a bunch, discarding the tougher leaves often just by snapping off the fibrous stems.

Bean Sprouts: The sprout revolution is up and growing! Radish sprouts, lentil sprouts, chickpea sprouts, soybean sprouts, and every other conceivable seed has been sprouted, especially for sale in health food stores. For the recipes in this book, the sprouts used are mung bean sprouts, the most commonly available. These are best purchased in an Asian market, since grocery varieties are almost consistently inferior.

As a child, I never ate bean sprouts with their roots or heads attached. The crystalline, refreshing sweetness of the stem alone was sought. It was the regular, everyday activity for cook to pick through a mess of sprouts, ridding them of heads and tails. Those days are gone, but it is possible to buy very succulent and plump sprouts which are mainly stem. Sprouts raised for and by the commercial Asian establishments are often this way. They are raised slowly and never see the light of day; conditions are controlled so that they reach upward, becoming plump, straight, and long but not leggy and tough. They then are cleaned so that very few green husks remain, and the long roots are eliminated. But whether you can get Asian sprouts or are limited to your local supermarket, take care in selecting them. If there is any hint of softening or any moisture around the stems, beware. Smell them if you can; there should be no odor but the suggestion of a faint sweetness, like the neutral freshness of a cucumber or apple.

Tofu: Also called bean curd, tofu is the precipitated, or jelled, custard of soybean milk. The way it is formed is comparable to separating the curds from whey of dairy milk—the solid protein comes out of the liquid. In the case of bean curds, they are formed into soft white blocks the consistency of custard.

For the recipes in this book, use only fresh tofu. Stale tofu will disappoint you, although some shopkeepers will insist that tofu is edible until it is spoiled. But this older tofu can taste terribly stale, and you should try to avoid any more than 2 or 3 days old. I always ask when the delivery arrives; then try to get to the store that day and buy the local product, not the brand that has been shipped from a long distance. About thirty minutes before cooking tofu, take it out of its container and place it in a big bowl of fresh water.

PASTAS AND PASTRIES

It has been claimed that all noodles (and pastas) originated in China. Whether or not this is true, there is no arguing the point that the Asian cuisines make diverse use of this type of food, in the most wonderful ways. They stretch and cut noodles into every conceivable size and shape. They fill wonton wrappers and stuff noodle doughs with a variety of mixtures. And they make their noodles and doughs from different kinds of flours—not just wheat flour, but also rice flour and flour made from mung beans. It is a world of food which beckons exploring and promises adventure. Moreover, many of the noodles can be purchased in a convenient dried form. The two traditions of pasta making and food drying combine to produce the best dried noodles of any cuisine.

The recipes in this book use both Asian noodles and Western-style noodles. Modern-day means of drying and packaging pasta vary from country to country, and you'll find subtle differences in the quality of pastas, which can make fascinating dinnertime comparisons. I find the Chinese noodles generally more tender and finer than the Italian forms; they cook quicker in water and soften very evenly, from the edges in. Perhaps it has to do with the type of flour used, with the forming of the dough, with the addition of bicarbonate of soda (in the Chinese version), or with the drying process. But you may react differently. Try the different types of noodles, and occasionally give an exhilarating twist to a familiar meal by crossing the cultural barriers. As long as you substitute wheat-for-wheat, you'll have success.

From Wheat: Available fresh or dried, wheat noodles come in several widths. The Japanese alimentary paste noodles (somen) are very much the same, and more common in the supermarkets. Italian pastas are also made from wheat, and come in myriad shapes and sizes; buy those made from durum wheat or semolina.

From Rice: Rice vermicelli (also sometimes called rice sticks) are usually sold dried, and come in varying widths. The thinnest are very stringlike, becoming white when cooked.

From Bean Flour: Cellophane noodles, also called bean threads, are thin and translucent but brittle when dry. Soak briefly in water to soften before cooking.

Wonton Wrappers: These are wheat-flour pastries, rolled flat and cut into rounds or squares. When made larger, they become eggroll wrappers. Many supermarkets now carry wonton and eggroll wrappers.

Spring Roll Wrappers: These are thin, eggless pastries made from wheat flour and sold either round or square. They are available in Asian markets, frozen and labeled as "spring roll wrappers"; other times, they are mislabeled "eggroll wrappers," with "spring rolls" in smaller print. The Philippines export this pastry too, and call it "lumpia." Once you have seen the spring roll wrappers, however, you will not mistake them for eggroll dough. Although extremely thin and porous, they are quite resilient. When a handful of the runny dough is smeared against a hot griddle, like dusting with a damp cloth, a film is left, cooked onto the griddle. This results in a fine membrane of starch, held together by a web of strong gluten strands. When deep-fried, these wrappers become much crisper than eggroll wrappers.

VINEGARS AND LIQUORS

Several vinegars are used in this book. Cider vinegar is your ordinary grocery-store type, suitable for recipes when no specific type of vinegar is indicated. Red wine vinegar and balsamic vinegars are both grape-based, the latter a popular vinegar that has only recently come to us from Italy. It is made from the Trebbiano di Spagna grape, cooked and aged in wooden casks. Balsamic vinegar is quite concentrated, but if you use it in small quantities, you will find it deeply aromatic. You can substitute balsamic vinegar whenever red wine vinegar is indicated, but only in conservative amounts.

Zijiang vinegar is a type of rice vinegar originating in the province of Zijiang. It is also often labeled "Chekiang vinegar" or "Chinkiang vinegar." Very dark and rich, this is an aged vinegar that is especially good with fish and shellfish. Other types of rice vinegars abound in Asian markets. They are all suitable for recipes in this book that call for rice vinegar. The Japanese brands are tasty, although you should avoid those seasoned with sugar and other flavors.

Pale dry sherry, and sometimes Madeira, is used in these recipes. Both are interchangeable with rice wine. Wine is used most often as a curing agent in Chinese cooking, as a means of ridding meat of its raw, sometimes gamey taste. When the flavor of the wine itself is important to the recipe, I specify rice wine, in which instance, saké (Japanese rice wine) can be used. A bottle of unpretentious sherry or Madeira will last a good long while and should be a regular item in your pantry.

GINGERROOT, GARLIC, AND SCALLIONS

Gingerroot: This is the rhizome of the ginger plant. By now it should be familiar to any cook, because supermarkets have been stocking it for years. A knobby hunk, gingerroot has a light brown skin. If you are rendering the ginger in oil, you need not peel it; simply slice off a ⅛-inch piece about the area of a teaspoon to equal a slice, as indicated in the recipes here. Ginger as a seasoning should be used sparingly, since it has a penetrating taste. Most often, however, it is used to flavor the oil in which the food will be stir-fried. Once rendered in the oil, remove and discard the piece of ginger.

Garlic: Normal cloves of garlic are familiar to most of us. Elephant garlic is used in this book, however, and it is much larger and not as strong in flavor. The two are interchangeable, unless elephant garlic is specified.

Scallions: Also commonly called "spring onions," scallions are members of the onion family. Choose scallions that are firm, fresh-looking, and moderately large. Avoid those with bulbous bottoms.

HOT PEPPERS

There are a number of spicy dishes in this book, many of which are made with hot peppers. The quantity you ultimately use is subject to your tastes and habits. Select fresh peppers when the recipe calls for them, and remember that the smaller a pepper, generally the hotter it is. Red peppers are also usually hotter than green ones, and the seeds and core of peppers contain most of the fire. Depending on the peppers available to you, you might be able to use the tiny ones from Southeast Asia, or the larger ones generally grown in this country. Whenever you work with hot peppers, be careful not to scratch or rub your eyes with fingers that have touched the peppers. Serve a plain starch, such as rice, to counter the peppers.

SAUCES, PASTES, AND OTHER "WET" SEASONINGS

There is a variety of flavorings that you can use to season your foods. These flavorings are an essential part of each recipe.

Bean Sauce: This is a mixture of naturally fermented soybeans, flour, and salt. From this mixture, soy sauce is also distilled. In other words, bean sauce is a brown, nutty, robust version of soy sauce, and you may find it still in bean form or with the beans mashed into a paste. If you have the bean form, simply press it with a fork to roughly mash it. Bean sauce is known also as *miso* in Japan, where they use barley and other grains in fermentation. Hot bean paste and garlic-chili paste are variations on the basic bean paste, in which red hot chilies and sometimes garlic are added.

Hoisin Sauce: This is also a bean-based sauce that is somewhat sweet and quite popular in southern regional Chinese food. It is very widely available.

Fish Sauce: Used extensively in Southeast Asian cooking, fish sauce is a clear brown liquid extracted from fish, salt, and water. I find it a versatile seasoning agent, not strong like anchovy paste. Correctly used, it heightens the flavors of everything from salad dressing to a sauté of beef or veal. Fish sauce can even spark a tomato sauce. Most Asian food markets carry this sauce, especially those dealing with products from Thailand, Vietnam, and the Philippines. I prefer the Thai brands.

Oyster Sauce: This is an ingredient for which the French have a better translation—*essence des huitres*—or, in other words, oyster essence or extract. Like fish sauce and soy sauce, this is a concentrated condiment which is used in moderate amounts to season foods; it is not a sauce to blanket a dish. Oyster sauce is not "fishy" in taste, and that is why it can be used with red meats and vegetables. Commonly available, you'll find oyster sauce in most Asian supermarkets.

Anchovy Paste: This is a book that crosses cultures, so I include recipes that feature anchovy paste. I recommend buying imported anchovy paste, which usually comes in a tube. In all the recipes calling for shrimp paste, you can substitute anchovy paste, although it is rather an inferior substitute and tastes pale next to the better Thai ingredient. However, anchovy paste is quite right in Veal and Sweet Basil, which is a dish of Italian seasonings that uses basil in a Thai fashion.

Shrimp Paste: Sun-dried and salt-cured, shrimp paste is made from whole shrimp and is a mainstay of Indonesian, Malay, Thai, and Vietnamese food. The name conjures up fishy, smelly, and unpleasant odors and tastes, but in fact, this is a wonderful seasoning, intensely concentrated but without necessarily suggesting the sea. It is inexpensive—I buy the Thai brands—and keeps well, but make sure you scrape off the thin layer of wax on the top.

Sirija Sauce: Also spelled *sriraja, sriracha,* and *sod siraja,* this premier hot sauce of Thailand is named after the town which made it famous. When we went to Sirija for weekends, we always came back with a bottle of the sauce. It is a finely balanced mixture of red pepper, vinegar, sugar, garlic, and salt. You may raise an eyebrow at the sugar, but like so many things Thai, sugar is the handmaiden of hot pepper. It is necessary to temper the spiciness, and is never actually sweet. Whenever hot sauce is mentioned in this book, siracha will outshine Tabasco and other hot sauces.

Curry Paste: In Thai cuisine, curry paste consists of pulverized dried herbs (sometimes roasted first), all relentlessly gnashed in their stone mortars along with fresh native herbs, roots, and leaves as well as the all-important shrimp paste. The herbs and greens from native soil and the art of blending are impossible to duplicate, even when some fresh herbs are available here. I recommend buying the exported, blended curry paste, Mae Sri brand. If you refresh this canned paste with extra garlic, shallots, shrimp paste, and/or fresh lemon grass, you will have an extremely authentic, fresh-tasting curry.

The canned pastes come in 4-ounce tins, and there are many varieties. In this book, the red and green pastes are used. You may initially have to look carefully to find these pastes because Thai words fill the labels, whereas English text is small.

If you prefer to start your curry paste from scratch, combine the following ingredients and blend in a mortar until smooth. This is Musaman Curry Paste.

> *1/2 cup each chopped shallots, garlic, and fresh lemon grass*
>
> *1 tablespoon each khaa* (laos) *and coriander root*
>
> *1 teaspoon grated magrut peel*
>
> *1 teaspoon ground black pepper*
>
> *10 to 20 red peppers, seeded*
>
> *1 tablespoon salt*
>
> *1 tablespoon coriander seeds*
>
> *1/2 teaspoon ground nutmeg and mace*
>
> *1/2 teaspoon ground cinnamon and cloves*
>
> *2 tablespoons shrimp paste*
>
> *2 to 3 cardamom seeds*

FRESH HERBS

The more common Western herbs are used in this book, and whenever possible, use fresh ones. Fresh parsley and dill are easy to obtain, but fresh thyme, rosemary, oregano, and savory take a bit more searching or a backyard herb garden.

Basil: Several types of fresh basil are used in these recipes. Sweet, large-leaved basil is easily found in the markets. Thai holy basil (*kaprow*) may be located in Asian or Southeast Asian markets. It is a medium leaf basil with a purple tint in the stems. I find purple or "opal" basil a satisfactory substitute.

Coriander: This is a fresh green-leaved herb which resembles parsley. It is often used in southern Chinese foods and extensively in Southeast Asian dishes. It is also prominent in Mexican cooking, known there as cilantro (with a larger-leaved variety). Certain supermarkets carry it in their produce sections. In Southeast Asian stores, the greens are sold whole, with the roots attached because the fresh root is prized for its flavor. The Thais pound the roots in their curry paste and use the leaves for garnish. I have found coriander seeds to be a satisfactory substitute for the root but not the leaves. When green and raw, the leaves have a strong flavor, and the uninitiated need to be warned about its pungent scent, which is an acquired taste.

Lemon Grass: This may be found fresh in Asian and Southeast Asian stores, but if you cannot get it fresh, buy the dried version and reconstitute it. Select the Southeast Asian dried lemon grass rather than American lemon grass.

Mint: There are a great many types of mint, and the variety sold in produce sections of stores is satisfactory for the recipes in this book. If you can get peppermint, I like its slight bite in the Thai Tartar and Ratatouille recipes.

SPICES

There are several spices used in this book, all of which are dried. These include five-spice powder, which is a blend of spices varying with the spice-maker but usually with cinnamon, anise, fennel, clove, and peppercorns. Sichuan peppercorns are sold whole and dried, but when cracked open, they have a distinctive aroma. Star anise is an eight-spoke seed pod, and the pod is favored rather than the seed in Chinese cooking. Anise and Sichuan peppercorns may be found in many ordinary supermarkets.

MISCELLANEOUS OTHER INGREDIENTS

Coconut Milk: There is much confusion about coconut milk. The liquid inside a coconut is actually coconut water, whereas the milk is the juice of pressed mature coconut meat. Coconut milk is a versatile food with as many uses as milk and cream. It gives body to sauces and gravies, contributes natural fat to a dish, thickens automatically when heated, and has an unforgetable sweet fragrance without a trace of sugar. It is absolutely crucial for any curry.

In Southeast Asia, bushel-sized wicker baskets of whole shelled coconut meat are sold. You must shell your own; buy a good-sized coconut heavy with liquid. Crack it open with a hammer or mallet and pry the meat from the shell. (I use a screwdriver; don't worry about the brown skin attached to the white flesh.) Grate the meat in a food processor or blender and add a little water if necessary. Then pour 2 cups of hot water over the grated coconut. Set a colander in a bowl and drape 2 pieces of cheesecloth over the colander. Pour the mush into it. Now squeeze the coconut solids, pressing out the milk. When allowed to settle for 30 minutes, the thicker cream will rise to the top, like fresh milk. Skim top layer for coconut cream.

Here's the good news. Canned coconut milk is now exported in large quantities by many of the Southeast Asian countries, especially Thailand and the Philippines. It comes unsweetened and it is quite acceptable in these recipes.

Dried Anchovies: These are often used as a seasoning and sometimes by themselves, as in Peanuts and Anchovies. While you are at an Asian market for the anchovies, buy raw peanuts too, because they are hard to find in most supermarkets. The anchovies are thin—paper-thin—and come packaged in cellophane bags.

Dried Mushrooms and Fungi: There are myriad varieties of mushrooms, but the most common are the Chinese dried black mushrooms. The Japanese shiitake can be substituted. Tree ears (used in *Banh Trang*) are a type of fungus, rather than a mushroom, with very little taste but with a crunchy texture. Both mushrooms and fungi must be soaked to soften before using; tree ears will expand three to four-fold.

Palm Sugar: Additional "coconut" character is given to any coconut dish if you use palm sugar. This Southeast Asian ingredient is a little difficult to come by; it is *gula malacca* in Indonesian—that is, sugar of the Malaccas. Desserts with this sugar will make visions of the South China Seas dance in your imagination. It is sugar in very raw form, with an absolutely seductive fragrance. It comes in brown blocks, sometimes biscuit size or much bigger and wrapped in coconut leaves. Pound it with a heavy kitchen tool to crumble it, and use it in Coconut Cream Custard.

Rock Sugar: This is sugar that has been crystallized into big chunks. The Chinese claim it is sweeter than granulated sugar, and they use it in recipes such as Glazed Soft-shelled Crabs. You can also substitute it for the granulated sugar in any of the braised dishes using soy sauce.

Sichuan Kohlrabi and Pickled Mustard Greens: These may both be purchased canned, although in Chinatowns in large cities, you can buy them loose from large ceramic vats. The trick is to know the look of these ingredients and to have in mind the various ways they are labeled. Sichuan kohlrabi is also sold as "Szechuan vegetable" and sometimes with the German name *gemeuse* or even "pickled vegetable." Pickled mustard greens are more often exported from Southeast Asia or southern China. They have a ribbed stalk that is wider than that of celery.

Some Wok Menus

There are no strict rules for composing menus, although there are some very good, time-proven practices. My menus reflect a blending of cuisines and influences. Certain menus move in a classic French progression from fish course to red meat, while others start with something quite sharp to pique the appetite, more in the Chinese tradition. I also suggest a noodle dish in second place, as do the Italians, when planning a longer menu. Finally, I seek balance and echos in some menus—coconut in the first course and coconut in the dessert, for example—and a little of the unexpected—a warm first course, a cold main course, a warm dessert course, for instance.

Often, the dessert listed is simply fresh fruit. Fruit as the conclusion to a meal is a light ending, not just for one's appetite and figure, but also for refreshing a complex meal of many courses. A platter of common and exotic fruits—kiwis, papaya slices, apples, pears, and grapes—can be very inviting. Many Asian markets now carry thumb-sized sweet bananas and various types of mangoes. A lovely plate and a paring knife per person can dress up the service. If the fruits are sweet and well chosen, there is no need to cut them up and mix into a salad; the platter of whole fruits can be beautiful by itself.

If your meal is more traditional, follow the movement of courses with wines that progress from light to robust. On the other hand, if your menu has a more Eastern flavor, accompany your first course, which will be spicy, with beer or a continuation of the drinks you served before dinner. Foods that are cooked in very hot oil often clash with wines that are too dry; for these you need a wine on the sweeter side or even a flavorful beer.

The menus indicate the combined preparation and cooking times, so the hours and minutes given for the larger, more complex menus cannot be exact because much depends on how much you can accomplish while another dish is cooking. A few recipes can be started days in advance, and many of the dishes requiring lengthy times are merely hours during which the food is cooked slowly, virtually unsupervised.

All recipes listed in the menus are included in the book (see index) unless the item appears without a page number; these latter items are standard cooking dishes such as salads and breads, and you should use your favorite recipe.

Quick Menus

Consommé
Chicken Rice with Cucumber Garnish *(page 112)*
Fresh Fruit or Ice Cream
(1 hour, 35 minutes)

Banh Trang *(page 102)*
or Fried Beans, Sichuan Style *(page 96)*
Smothered Veal Chops *(page 191)*
Rice
Cheese and Fruit
(1 hour, 5 minutes)

Breaded Pork Cutlets *(page 17)*
Feta cheese Stir-fried Spinach *(page 81)*
Apples and Gorgonzola Cheese
or Almond Cream Omelette *(page 202)*
(45 minutes; 1 hour, 10 minutes with omelette)

Peanuts and Crisp Anchovies *(page 62)*
45-Minute Lasagna *(page 128)*
Green Salad
Wine and fruit
(1 hour)

Light Menus

These light menus turn out even faster than the quick menus.

Brown Chicken *(page 143)*
Rice
Sprouts Stir-fried with Green Peppers *(page 85)*
Sherbet or Fresh Fruit
(45 minutes)

Steamed Vegetables with Lean Spicy Dip *(page 54)*

Lobster on a Bed of Basil *(page 168)*
Rice or Bread and Butter

Fresh Fruit

(50 minutes)

Warm Sprout Salad *(page 101)*

Steamed Sole Vinaigrette *(page 173)*
Rice

Grand Marnier Omelette

(1 hour)

Thai Tartare *(page 108)*

Chicken and Prosciutto *(page 184)*
Rice, Buttered Noodles, or Bread and Butter

Fruit and Wine

(45 minutes)

Fix-Ahead Menus

The main dishes for these menus are quick braising or steaming dishes that can be reheated or prepared in advance.

Vegetables with Spicy Sauce *(page 52)*

Thai Chicken in Green Curry *(page 145)*
Rice

Steamed Coconut Cream Custard *(page 203)*
or Fresh Fruit

(1 hour, 15 minutes; 1 hour, 45 minutes with custard)

Savory Garlic Cheesecake *(page 75)*
or Thai Tartare *(page 108)*

Butter-glazed Chicken and Onions *(page 144)*
Rice

Green Salad

Almond Shortcake with Candied Pumpkin *(page 214)*

(2 hours, 45 minutes)

Braised Shrimp *(page 134)*

Quick Cannelloni *(page 130)*
or Pork-Stuffed Zucchini with Italian Sauce *(page 152)*
Rice

Green Salad

Apple Sherbet with Apple Flan *(page 206)*

(3 hours, 45 minutes)

French-fried Carrots with Garlic-Pickle Sauce *(page 98)*

Meatcake with Salt Cod, Served with Steamed Buns *(page 140)*
Feta Cheese Stir-fried Spinach *(page 81)*

Nut Torte

(2 hours, 45 minutes)

Formal Menus

*Many of these recipes may be prepared in advance. There may be some overlap—
you can prepare one while another is cooking. Refer to the specific recipes for ideas
about advance procedures.*

A Caviar Nest *(page 48)*

Eastern Steak *(page 194)*
Culled Broccoli with Anchovy and Garlic Sauce *(page 90)*
French-fried Carrots with Garlic-Pickle Sauce *(page 98)*

Cheeses, Fruit

(2 hours, 20 minutes)

Glazed Soft-shelled Crabs *(page 60)*

Pasta Satchels with Ricotta Filling *(page 64)*

Lobster Chinoise *(page 166)*
Rice

Green Salad

Snow-topped Cream *(page 208)*

(3½ hours)

Mussels with Basil and Cream *(page 56)*

Whole Crispy Chicken *(page 180)*
Rice or Noodles
Carrot Roux *(page 83)*

Buttered Green Peas

Green Salad

Steamed Coconut Cream Custard *(page 203)*

(3 hours, 45 minutes)

Peanuts and Crisp Anchovies *(page 62)*
Sausage and Oysters in Lettuce Leaves *(page 104)*

Thai Crisp Vermicelli *(page 198)*

Rice Crumb Steamed Pork *(page 196)*
French-fried Beans Provencale *(page 94)*

Poached Bananas with Coconut Cream *(page 203)*

(5 hours, 20 minutes)

Seasonal Menus

SPRING

Snow Pea Greens *(page 88)*
or Carrot Roux *(page 83)*

Steamed Sole Vinaigrette (without spinach) *(page 173)*
Asparagus
Rice

Cheese and Bread

Strawberries and Crème Fraîche

(1 hour)

SUMMER

Provencale Peppers *(page 82)*

Beef and Basil *(page 74)*
or Veal and Sweet Basil *(page 190)*
Rice

Blueberry Pudding *(page 210)*

(1 hour, 35 minutes; 1 hour, 55 minutes for veal)

FALL

Pork and Fish in Banana Pepper Boats *(page 156)*
or Stuffed Acorn Squash *(page 80)*

Lamb with Turnips and Greens *(page 157)*
with Rice or Buttered Noodles;
or Salmon in Bombay Gin *(page 176)*
with French Bread

Mussels with Basil and Cream

PAGES 56-57

Scallop Kebabs

PAGE 55

Cheese
Poached Pears with Hard Sauce *(page 209)*
(4 hours, 30 minutes)

THANKSGIVING OR HOLIDAY MENU
Carved Squash Soup *(page 178)*
Whiskeyed Turkey *(page 49)*
Veal Roulades with Orange Peel *(page 192)*
or Grilled Spicy Duck *(page 188)*
Rice
Culled Broccoli with Anchovy and Garlic Sauce *(page 90)*
Carrot Roux *(page 83)*
Apple Sherbet with Apple Custard *(page 206)*
(6 hours)

WINTER
Asparagus Timbale *(page 76)*
Beef and Garlic *(page 148)*
Rice
Sprouts Stir-fried with Green Peppers *(page 85)*
Chocolate Omelette *(page 201)*
(2 hours, 15 minutes)

Cocktail Parties

Spring Rolls with Banh Trang Dip *(pages 66, 102)*
Stuffed Chicken Wings *(page 72)*
Whiskeyed Turkey *(page 49)* with Toasted Triangles
Steamed Vegetables with a Lean Spicy Dip *(page 54)*
Savory Garlic Cheesecake *(page 75)*
Braised Shrimp *(page 134)*
(6 hours)

Light Pâté *(page 51)* with crackers
Melted Cheese Triangles *(page 63)*
Banh Trang *(page 102)*
Scallop kebabs *(page 55)*
Peanuts and Crisp Anchovies *(page 62)*
Fresh Fruit
Cheese
(3½ hours)

Spareribs Gorgonzola *(page 71)*
Steamed Vegetables with a Lean, Spicy Dip *(page 54)*
Brie and crackers
Oysters Americaine *(page 59)*
Pasta Satchels *(page 64)*
(3½ hours)

Appetizers, Vegetables, and Other Small Courses

The recipes in this chapter may be served in a number of flexible settings. By "small course" I mean a vegetable side dish, a piece of meat, a pasta, a condiment, or even a luncheon dish. Often a small course functions as a traditional first course or a soup, but actually this is a wonderfully open-ended category.

These small courses are the Italian *antipasta,* the Spanish *tapas,* Chinese cold and hot openers, and familiar *hors d'oeuvre.* They are food to tarry over, to sip with wine, to nibble as you chat. You can manipulate the service to your liking. A simple meal, or a meal to be served within time limits, means one small course—perhaps a more substantial selection. If you wish to stretch out the evening, then offer a string of small courses, one after another. If you want variety and a more elaborate presentation but mind the time, put out three or four at one time.

Although for some people to melt into a soft, deep chaise with a drink in hand is ultimate relaxation, it can be difficult to serve and eat food from semi-reclined positions. And the effort of juggling a plate, cocktail napkin, and drink on one's knees spoils the enjoyment of the food. Moreover I think it a pity to cut off the variety of dinner openers and appetizers because of the limitations of finger food. Food passed around moreover is never really hot or cold enough. That is why I often use a modified Chinese strategy. Appetizers are eaten at the table, and both hands are free for drink, utensils, napkin, and food. Your guests are seated comfortably, although not ensconced. Drinks are poured and served in the living room, time allowed to flow, and then guests are invited to bring their drinks to the table where appetizers are. From there, drink orders change to wine very smoothly as people finish cocktails at their own pace. The transition from living room to table and from appetizer to dinner moves smoothly and elegantly.

The concept of small courses offers another advantage. The manner of serving and the quantity served will change the character of a course. A vegetable dish such as Feta Cheese and Spinach may be a side dish; a little more of it, along with some toast triangles, and you can serve it as a first course—perhaps in the position where a salad might go. Make even more of it, serve it with crusty warm bread, and you have a light lunch. Two other examples are the Spring Rolls and the Pasta Satchels. You may pass them at a stand-up affair, put a handful on a dish for a first course, or serve several on a plate for a small meal.

The recipes that follow encompass both cold and hot dishes, finger foods (because they are still a necessity and convenience of modern entertaining), vegetable selections (including but not exclusively accompaniments to main dishes), warm salads, and wrap-up foods (do-it-yourself dishes). Mix and match as you wish, and choose the dishes that suit the purpose you have in mind. Enjoy!

Artichokes and Mayonnaise in a Waterlily Setting

This recipe makes a pretty presentation. Cayenne or paprika is used to flavor the mayonnaise and color it a subtle peach. Present these as individual servings or cluster them on a large and beautiful serving platter.

SERVES 4 AS A FIRST COURSE

1 **PRE-STEAM**

Bring water to a boil in wok, with rack in place.

2 **CUT**
4 medium artichokes
½ lemon

With a serrated stainless-steel knife, cut the bottom of each artichoke so it will sit stable. Peel off bottom leaves. Trim remaining top leaves. Rub cut parts with the lemon. Place artichokes on a steaming dish, or directly on the rack if it is perforated.

3 **STEAM**

Steam artichokes over high heat for 20 to 30 minutes or until a leaf may be easily tugged off. Add hot water to wok when necessary. When done, immediately cool artichokes with running water. Set aside.

4 **MIX**
3 cups mayonnaise, homemade or jarred
¼ teaspoon fish sauce
1 tablespoon cayenne or paprika

Mix mayonnaise with seasonings, then refrigerate for at least 30 minutes.

5 **ASSEMBLE**

Squeeze excess water from artichokes. Open up the leaves and remove the chokes; scrape away the stubborn ones with a stainless-steel spoon. Press the leaves so the artichokes are like pretty blossoms, then spoon or spiral (with pastry bag and large star tip) some mayonnaise mixture into the centers. For a large arrangement, place 1 artichoke on the platter and remove enough leaves so that it suggests a tight flower bud. Spread the remainder of the mayonnaise onto a large, flat platter in the shape of a leaf or several leaves. Strategically cluster the artichoke blossoms and bud at the base of the leaves. Serve chilled or at room temperature, with extra mayonnaise on the side.

A Caviar Nest

Bean threads are very fine, shimmering clear noodles made from mung bean flour. Both the bean threads and egg slivers may be made in advance. Form the "nest" on one large serving plate, or make several smaller nests on individual plates.

SERVES 4 AS AN APPETIZER

---

1 **SOAK**
2 cups bean threads (a 2-ounce package)

Soak noodles in cold water until no longer brittle, about 20 minutes. Drain.

---

2 **MAKE CREPES**
8 tablespoons butter
4 eggs, lightly beaten

Place 2 tablespoons butter in wok and add a small ladleful of egg. Make a large, thin crêpe and cook until just set. Remove while still soft, and roll into a cylinder. Continue to make 3 more crêpes, adding 2 tablespoons butter to pan each time. When crêpes are cool, cut cylinders into slivers ever so fine.

---

3 **COOK**
4 cups chicken stock or water

Bring stock to a boil in a 2-quart saucepan and plunge in the drained noodles. Cook 2 minutes or until soft. Drain and cool with running water immediately.

---

4 **CUT AND TOSS**
3 tablespoons walnut or olive oil

Using scissors, cut the bean threads into 1-inch segments. Place in the serving dish and toss with oil.

---

5 **ARRANGE**
1/2 to 1 cup caviar (salmon, Icelandic lumpfish, or whatever you can afford)

Make a nest of the noodles on the serving dish. Line the nest with the egg slivers. (You can cover the nest with plastic wrap and refrigerate until ready to serve.) Pile caviar in the middle and serve.

Whiskeyed Turkey

This is a cold dish, entertaining to serve. Pieces of lightly steamed turkey are permeated with bourbon or whiskey. But don't be alarmed—the meat does not taste drowned in the liquor; rather, the perfume delicately scents every fiber of the meat and the juices meld into a mellow brine—not at all harsh.*

SERVES 8 AS AN APPETIZER, 4 AS A MAIN COURSE

---

1 **BONE**
½ *turkey breast*
1 *tablespoon salt*

De-bone the turkey breast. Cut into 4 pieces. Rub all over with the salt. Place on a steaming plate.

---

2 **STEAM**

Bring water to a boil in wok, with rack in place. Steam turkey breast on high heat for 25 to 30 minutes or until the meat is just done. Do not overcook. Let cool in its juices.

---

3 **ASSEMBLE AND MARINATE**
¾ *cup bourbon*

In a deep bowl, mix the steaming juices and the bourbon. Place the turkey meat in the liquid, cover with plastic wrap, and refrigerate for 3 days. Turn the pieces once a day.

---

4 **SERVE**

Drain and cut turkey into ¼-inch slices. Spoon the slightly congealed sauce over them, and serve cold, with triangle croutons. Or consider including this on a cocktail buffet table with toasted bread on the side.

---

*Improvisation not recommended; use all measurements as given.

Light Pâté with Beer and Brown Peppercorns

 This is a rustic pâté. By light I mean light meat as well as light on time, expense, calories, and seasonings. Sichuan brown peppercorns are the main flavoring. The layer of fat which is usually wrapped around a pâté is eliminated, and the moisture replaced by beer. The pâté is light because it is cooked by the slight touch of steam.

SERVES 8 TO 10 AS A FIRST COURSE

1 **MINCE**
2 pounds turkey meat, about ½ turkey breast
1½ pounds boneless pork, preferably Boston butt
¼ pound chicken fat

Cut turkey, pork, and chicken fat into small pieces. If you have a food processor, spin the pork and chicken fat together, then add turkey. You should have a fine-textured grind but not a paste. If you are using a meat grinder, put meats and fat through the grind twice. Place meat in a bowl.

2 **ADD**
2 cloves garlic
1½ teaspoons Sichuan peppercorns
1½ cups beer
2 tablespoons whiskey
2 teaspoons salt
½ teaspoon cayenne

Put the garlic through a press. Crush the peppercorns and mix with the rest of the ingredients into the meat mixture. Put mixture into a 6-cup loaf pan or shallow round mold.

3 **STEAM**

Bring water to a boil in wok, with rack in place. Steam over high heat for 5 minutes, then lower heat and steam pâté over medium-low heat (water at a simmer) for 1½ to 2 hours. Check once or twice to make sure there is plenty of water. Re-fill the wok with boiling water when the level is low. Pâté is done when the juices run a clear yellowish liquid. Pierce the meat with a knife and press down to bring the liquid out.

4 **PRESS**

When pâté is done, take out of the steamer and pour off excess liquid. Cover with plastic wrap, then press down by using foil-covered bricks, heavy cans of food or jars of water. Refrigerate overnight, weighted.

5 **SERVE**

Remove weights, scrape off the fat and slightly congealed juices, then cut into ⅝-inch-thick slices and serve with a spoonful of the juices over the slices.

Chicken Liver Rillettes

The way these livers are prepared is much like rillettes, *the French potted pork. These "rillettes" cook much faster in a wide steaming dish set into a wok than if potted in a deep pan, as the pork would be.*

SERVES 4 TO 6 AS AN APPETIZER

---

1 **GRIND AND MINCE**
1/4 pound salt pork
3/4 pound chicken livers
1/4 pound chicken fat
1 bunch scallions

Rinse salt off pork and cut away the rind; slice 1/8 inch thick. Coarse grind the slices along with the chicken livers and chicken fat in a meat grinder, processor, or by hand. Mince the white parts of the scallions. Combine all in a bowl.

---

2 **SEASON**
1/4 cup brandy
1 1/2 tablespoons garlic-chili paste
1 tablespoon red wine vinegar
2 tablespoons minced fresh parsley
1/4 teaspoon dried thyme
1/4 teaspoon salt
pinch of black pepper
1/4 teaspoon cayenne
2 to 3 bay leaves

Add all seasonings, except bay leaves, to the liver mixture and mix well.

Pour into a steaming dish or a shallow mold with sides no deeper than 1 1/2 inches. Arrange the bay leaves attractively over the liver mixture.

---

3 **STEAM**

Bring water to a boil in a wok with rack in place. Place steaming dish on rack and steam over high heat for 2 minutes, then reduce to a simmer and steam for 25 to 30 minutes. Replenish the wok with simmering water when necessary.

---

4 **SERVE**

Allow the dish to cool, then refrigerate. It is better when allowed to mellow a day or two. You may transfer the mixture to a deeper "pot" before refrigerating if you wish, or just leave it to serve from the wide flared ceramic steaming dish. Serve as a spread with toast or crackers.

Vegetables with Spicy Sauce

 Raw vegetables and a dip are a staple at stand-up affairs, from cocktail parties to buffet dinners. This recipe, based on the sauces of Thailand, Indonesia, Malay, and other Southeast Asian countries, is a radical, refreshing departure from the common cheese-based dips.

The combination of vegetables could also be transformed into a salad. Compose a potpourri of raw and steamed vegetables with this sauce as a salad dressing. Vegetables you might steam are okra, broccoli, and all manner of beans. For raw vegetables, try cauliflower, bean sprouts, cucumber, jicama, leafy greens such as Belgian endive, escarole, spinach, and sorrel. Or dispense with the usual and set out a basket of cold, steamed new potatoes and sweet potato wedges.

SERVES 8 AS AN APPETIZER

1 **WASH AND CUT** *approximately ¹/₂ pound each new potatoes or regular potatoes, sweet potatoes, green or wax beans, and zucchini*	Leave tiny new potatoes whole; cut larger ones in half. Slice full-size white potatoes and sweet potatoes ⁵/₈ inch thick and then quarter the slices. Trim the beans. Cut the squash into rounds or sticks.
2 **STEAM**	Set up a wok for steaming. Heat the water and let boil. Place the prepared vegetables on bamboo or metal trays for steaming, or place on plates. (Do not stack vegetables; 1 layer per container.) The potatoes take longest to steam—about 15 minutes. Pierce with knife to test if tender. The beans and squash take less time; they should be tender but still firm in about 2 minutes. When beans are cooked, immediately shower with cold water to cool.
3 **PUREE** *3 cloves garlic* *3 shallots* *4 fresh cayenne or jalapeño peppers* *2 teaspoons shrimp paste*	Peel the garlic and shallots. Core, seed, and slice hot peppers. Place ingredients in a food processor or pound in a mortar until you have a paste.
4 **FRY** *4 tablespoons oil*	Heat oil in wok over high heat. Stir in the paste, turning the mixture with the spatula at a moderate pace until fragrant.

5 **ADD**

*2 cups coconut milk,
either canned or
fresh*

*¹/₃ cup unsweetened
peanut butter*

1 tablespoon sugar

*1 tablespoon soy
sauce*

*1 teaspoon lime
juice*

Pour coconut milk into wok, and turn the mixture. It will thicken after it boils. If too thick, add water; it should be the consistency of a light batter. Add sugar and lime juice, then turn off heat. Pour sauce into a bowl and place next to vegetables, or pour dressing over individual salads.

Steamed Vegetables with a Lean, Spicy Dip

 Here is another vegetable dip that is very lean indeed. It comes from the Thai nam-prik, which is a thin sauce that is tasty and very fiery, though in this recipe you can adjust the amount of hot pepper to your taste. It can serve as a dip for a medley of raw and steamed vegetables (see preceding recipe) or with batter-fried vegetables. Or toss the dip into steamed vegetables as a dressing and serve as a warm salad.

SERVES 4 TO 6 AS AN APPETIZER

1 | **PREPARE VEGETABLES** | See the preceding recipe for directions on preparing and steaming the vegetables.

1/2 pound each potatoes, green beans, zucchini, or other vegetables

2 | **ROAST** | Wrap shrimp paste in foil and place in a hot oven for 10 minutes.

1 tablespoon shrimp paste

3 | **PUREE** | Use a food processor or blender to purée ingredients, or pound in a mortar until you have a smooth paste. Add roasted shrimp paste and blend well.

3 cloves garlic
1 teaspoon salt
2 to 6 fresh cayenne or jalapeño peppers, seeded
1 Granny Smith apple, peeled and sliced; or 1 cup cranberries

4 | **SEASON** | Stir seasonings into purée. Add a little more sugar if the sauce has too much bite. (Sugar can reduce the perception of hotness by a few degrees.)

1/2 cup fish sauce
5 tablespoons sugar, approximately
3 tablespoons lime juice

5 | **SERVE** | Have plain white rice or white bread on hand to quell the heat for the innocent. Garnish the dip by floating some mint, coriander, or watercress leaves on top.

Scallop Kebabs

Pearly bay scallops, a ribbon of ham, and a small green pea fit perfectly on a toothpick. The kebab is gently steamed and then coated with a glistening glaze just before serving.*

SERVES 4 TO 6 AS AN APPETIZER

---

1 DEFROST
  1/3 cup frozen shelled
     peas

Break up frozen peas and set aside.

---

2 MARINATE
  1 teaspoon light soy
     sauce
  2 teaspoons sherry
  2 teaspoons cornstarch
  1/2 pound bay scallops

Pour the seasonings over the scallops and mix. Leave for 30 minutes to 1 hour, then drain and reserve marinade.

---

3 CUT
  1/4 pound boiled ham

Buy the ham sliced paper thin. Cut slices into strips 1/2 inch wide and 3 inches long.

---

4 SKEWER

Using a toothpick, lance the ingredients in this order: scallop, ham, scallop, pea. Snake the toothpick through the length of ham with 3 to 4 loops, then compress it slightly like a coiled spring. You should make 16 to 20 skewers.

---

5 STEAM

Heat water in wok, with rack in place. Place the toothpick skewers in one layer on a steaming plate. Steam over high heat for 3 to 5 minutes, or just until the scallops become firm to the touch.

---

6 BOIL
  1/2 cup chicken stock
  2 teaspoons apple
     brandy
  pinch of white pepper
  salt to taste
  2 teaspoons
     cornstarch

Place stock, brandy, pepper, and salt in a saucepan. Pour in liquid from around the scallops. Add cornstarch and, while still cold, stir thoroughly to incorporate the cornstarch. Place over medium heat and continue stirring until the liquid boils and thickens. When it has turned clear, the sauce is ready.

---

7 SERVE

With a large pastry brush, generously paint the kebabs with the sauce. You may also serve these in a warming dish placed over a small Sterno flame, with the sauce poured around the kebabs.

---

*Improvisation not recommended; use all measurements as given.

Mussels with Basil and Cream

The herb and spice purée in this recipe is essentially a Thai curry paste; if some of these ingredients are unavailable, you can substitute ¼ can of Thai curry paste and refresh it with garlic, shallots, and coriander.*

SERVES 4 AS A FIRST COURSE, 2 AS A MAIN DISH WITH RICE

1
STEAM
1 cup basil leaves
2 to 3 pounds
  mussels

Bring water to a boil in wok, with rack in place. Steam the basil leaves over high heat just until they wilt. Refresh under cold water immediately, then drain and wring out excess moisture. Scrub the mussels well and remove beards. Place in a shallow dish in 1 layer, and steam until open. Remove the meat and save about ¼ of the largest pairs of shells.

2
PUREE
4 shallots
4 cloves garlic
2 tablespoons
  minced fresh
  lemongrass; or
  dried, soaked in
  cold water for 30
  minutes
1 teaspoon
  coriander root; or
  ½ cup chopped
  coriander leaves
½ teaspoon grated
  lime zest
1 to 4 dried hot red
  peppers, seeded
1½ teaspoons shrimp
  paste

Place shallots, garlic, and herbs in a food processor or blender and blend until a paste.

3
STIR-FRY
1 tablespoon oil

Heat oil in wok. Stir and turn the paste in the oil until the fragrances fill your sinuses. Remove to a small bowl.

4
MIX
1 cup fresh coconut
  milk, or 1 can
  (14-ounces)
  unsweetened
1½ tablespoons
  cornstarch
½ egg

If using canned milk, pour the contents into a bowl and remove about ⅓ cup of liquid; the cream has usually separated and hardened so that it is quite easy to separate the "whey." Mix coconut cream, cornstarch, and egg with the fried paste.

5 **ASSEMBLE**
1 hot red pepper,
   seeded and cut in
   thin slices
zest of 1 lime
1/4 cup tiny fresh
   coriander leaves

Place the empty shells onto a flat plate or wicker tray. In the bottom of each shell place 1 basil leaf. Lay 2 to 3 cooked mussels on top, and spoon the paste to fill the shell. Garnish with slices of red pepper and strips of lime zest. Break off single coriander leaf and arrange attractively on top.

6 **STEAM**

Bring water to a boil in wok, with rack in place. Steam mussels over medium heat for 7 to 10 minutes. As soon as cream mixture has set, dish is done.

Improvisation not recommended; use all measurements as given.

Steamed Oysters

 If oysters are to be cooked at all, they should be steamed. The gentle, moist cooking results in plump oysters that have been showered by the seasonings and herbs which drip downward with the condensed steam. This recipe uses traditional Chinese flavors; the next is more Western.

SERVES 2 TO 4 PEOPLE

1 **SOAK**
1 tablespoon salted
black beans

Soak beans in cold water while you proceed with the cutting and slicing.

2 **CUT AND TRIM**
2 scallions
½ cup packed fresh
coriander leaves
(optional)
2 cloves garlic

Cut scallions into 2-inch segments. With the point of a sharp knife, cut each segment lengthwise in half, then sliver each half. Pick leaves off coriander and float the scallion slivers and coriander leaves in a bowl of cold water with a handful of ice cubes. Mince the garlic as finely as possible. Drain the black beans and mince them to the same size as the garlic.

3 **MIX**
1 teaspoon soy sauce
2 teaspoons sherry
1 teaspoon sugar
2 tablespoons oil

In a small bowl, combine the soy sauce, sherry, sugar, and oil with the garlic and black beans. Set aside.

4 **PREPARE**
12 to 18 oysters, or
½ pint shucked

Open oysters with a knife, or steam them open. Bring water in wok to a boil, with rack in place. To open oysters, place on a plate or directly on a perforated steaming rack. Steam over high heat for about 5 minutes or until they barely crack open. Remove from wok and discard top shells. If using shucked oysters, place them in scallop shells on a shallow gratin dish; do not overlap.

5 **STEAM**

Spoon seasonings over each oyster. Drain coriander and garlic and strew over the oysters. Steam oysters over high heat for about 3 to 5 minutes if using fresh oysters, about 5 to 10 minutes if using shucked. Touch the tops; they should be hot and firm but not shrunken. Serve immediately.

Peanuts and Crisp Anchovies

PAGE 62

Pasta Satchels

PAGE 64

Oysters Americaine

A blanket of bright, finely minced greens and herbs covers each oyster; it is my wok version of Oysters Rockefeller.

SERVES 4 AS A FIRST COURSE, 2 AS A MAIN COURSE WITH WARMED BREAD

1 **BLEND**
1/4 *cup blanched almonds*
1/2 *cup unsalted butter, very cold*
1/4 *cup each chopped fresh chives, basil, parsley, and scallions*
1 *cup packed fresh spinach*
2 *cloves garlic*

Grind the almonds to a powder in a processor or blender. Slice butter thinly, then put butter and herbs into blender or processor. Spin until greens are finely chopped.

2 **STEAM**
12 to 18 oysters; or
1/2 *pint shucked*
1/2 *lemon*

Bring water to a boil in the wok, with steaming rack in place. To open oysters, place on a steaming plate or directly on a perforated steaming rack. Steam over high heat for about 5 minutes or just until they open. Take off steam and discard top shells. Place shucked oysters in scallop shells or on a shallow gratin dish; do not overlap. Squeeze a few drops of lemon juice on each oyster, then place about 1½ teaspoons of sauce on each, completely covering surface. Steam over high heat for 3 to 5 minutes if using fresh oysters and 5 to 10 minutes if using shucked. They should be hot and firm but not shrunken. Serve immediately.

Glazed Soft-shelled Crabs

These crabs are deep-fried without batter. The instant they come from the fat, and while their pores are hot and opened, they are glazed in an aromatic mixture. The crab is awash with flavor, every fiber penetrated by a rich soy and spice sauce that has a sweet edge. The Chinese use this method of preparing fish and call it xun (smoked), meaning that the high temperature and penetration of the seasonings is comparable to smoking.

SERVES 4 TO 8 PEOPLE AS AN APPETIZER

---

1 | **CUT**
4 soft-shelled crabs | Bisect the body of the crab, then cut again into 2. For each crab, you will have 4 pieces of body with 2 or 3 legs attached to each section.

---

2 | **MARINATE**
2 scallions
2 slices gingerroot
3 tablespoons dark soy sauce
2 tablespoons light soy sauce
1 tablespoon sherry
a 1-inch stick of cinnamon | Cut scallions into 2-inch sections. Lightly crush them and the ginger slices. Place in a bowl with the crab and seasonings, and leave for 3 to 4 hours.

---

3 | **HEAT**
2 cups oil | Heat oil for deep-frying until about 350 degrees.

---

4 | **BOIL**
3 lumps rock sugar; or ⅓ cup granulated
1 cup water
a 1-inch stick of cinnamon
1 star anise
1 teaspoon five-spice powder | While oil is heating, combine and boil sugar, water, and spices in a small saucepan until mixture thickens slightly. Turn heat down, and simmer glaze over low heat while you fry crabs.

| 5 | **DEEP-FRY AND GLAZE** | When oil is hot, drop 3 crab pieces into wok and deep-fry. Be careful; pockets of moisture in the crabs may explode. Each piece will take only 2 to 3 minutes to cook. As each piece finishes, take out of oil and dunk immediately into the simmering glaze. Let each piece soak up glaze, then remove after 1 to 2 minutes. Fry and glaze continuously. Remove from glaze onto a serving plate. |

| 6 | **SERVE** | Let crab pieces cool. These may be picked up by the legs to be eaten as finger food; they go splendidly with drinks. |

Peanuts and Crisp Anchovies

✳ *You may have seen packages of dried little minnows on the shelves of Asian groceries. The tiny, silvery anchovies are so new their skins are transparent. A staple of Southeast Asian cookery, these fish are used to flavor and season in every conceivable way. Quickly fried in oil, they crisp and decorate a dish, at the same time imparting flavor and aroma. They do not taste fishy, but rather are clean and savory.*

This recipe for crisped fish and peanuts, which I like to call "swimming peanuts," was originally served as a condiment for curry. The Raffles Hotel in Singapore—of Kipling and Maugham fame—serves its curry buffet with this for a side dish, but it is so good by itself, especially with drinks. The proportions are adjustable. If you feel conservative about the fish, make it a peanut dish with a touch of the crisp anchovies. Later, you will want to adjust it so there are more anchovies.

Total cooking time occupies no more than 5 minutes. Have the stove exhaust turned on and a window cracked open. Be ready with the perforated ladle, and be fleet of hand, since the anchovies are thin and burn very quickly. Leftover anchovies will keep forever since they are dried, but so that there is no loss of flavor, store them in the freezer.*

SERVES 8 AS AN HORS D'OEUVRE

1 **DEEP-FRY**
2 cups oil
1 cup dried
   anchovies
2 cups raw peanuts

Heat oil. (In the meantime, have a heatproof container ready to hold the boiling oil, with a funnel in place.) Pour in the dried fish all at once. Within 5 seconds, they will have turned a shade darker. Scoop them all out and set aside. Pour peanuts into the same oil. Stir them around with the perforated ladle. When they begin to turn golden, catch them with the ladle, and set aside. Immediately drain the oil through the funnel, leaving 3 tablespoons oil in wok.

2 **BOIL**
1/3 cup sugar
2 tablespoons cider
   vinegar
1 teaspoon red
   pepper flakes

Pour sugar, vinegar, and red pepper into wok. Stir to dissolve sugar, then let mixture boil and thicken. The sugar will begin to caramelize.

3 **COMBINE-FRY**

As soon as the sauce thickens, pour in the peanuts and fish. Stir to coat with the sauce, then scoop out immediately.

4 **SERVE**

Pass mixture around the table with other light items—marinated vegetables, for example. It is superb with cocktails, and makes a nice transition from drinks to dinner.

*Improvisation not recommended; use all measurements as given.

Melted Cheese Triangles

Melted cheese is one of the supreme taste treats. In this recipe, thin wonton pastries serve as the "carrier" for melted cheese. Wrapped around a piece of good cheese, sealed into a triangular package, and dipped into hot fat, they are crisp on the outside and have a package of warm melted cheese on the inside.

SERVES 8 TO 10 AS AN HORS D'OEUVRE

1 **CUT**
¼ *pound Swiss,*
  mozzarella, brie,
  camembert, or
  other melting
  cheese
2 cups packed fresh
  dill or chives

Cut cheese into strips ¼ inch thick and 1 inch long. You should have about 30 strips. Snip the herbs into 1-inch sections.

2 **WRAP**
20 to 30 wonton
  wrappers
1 egg, beaten

Keep the wrappers covered with a damp cloth as you work. Brush a ½-inch-wide strip of beaten egg on 2 adjoining sides of the square. Place cheese strip and 1 piece of herb in the middle, then fold the pastry square, forming a triangle, and press the edges together firmly. Form remaining triangles.

3 **DEEP-FRY**
2 cups oil

Heat oil in wok to 350 degrees. Slide in 3 or 5 triangles at a time and deep-fry. When the underside is lightly tanned, turn over. Scoop out with the perforated ladle and drain on paper towels. Continue to cook remaining triangles. Serve hot.

Pasta Satchels

A wonton wrapper is essentially a square of fresh pasta or noodle dough. In the form of a small square sheet, it can wrap a customary wonton. Or it can be a thin egg pastry casing for a little mouthful of delight. These steamed satchels are like open-faced sandwiches or canapés, perfect for passing around at a cocktail party. But it is also possible to place them prettily—six or eight each—on a plate and bathe them with a spoonful of tomato sauce for a first course.*

SERVES 10 TO 15 AS AN HORS D'OEUVRE

---

1   **SELECT FILLING**

Three possible fillings are given here. Select the one you prefer, or make all 3.

Sausage and Olive
1 pound bulk Italian sausage
1/2 cup pitted cured black olives
3 tablespoons tomato paste
2 tablespoons Madeira wine

Re-chop the sausage meat to make it a fine grind. Combine with remaining ingredients and blend well. Set aside.

Veal
1 tablespoon oil
3/4 cup chopped onion
1 pound ground veal or pork
salt and pepper
1 teaspoon brandy

Heat wok, add oil, and stir-fry the onion in wok over medium heat until onion is well-softened and excess moisture is evaporated. Cool, then mix with meat, seasonings and brandy. Set aside.

Ricotta-spinach
3/4 pound ricotta
1/2 package (10 ounces) chopped spinach, drained
3/4 cup grated parmesan cheese
1/4 cup bread crumbs, about
1 tablespoon chopped Italian parsley
salt and pepper
cayenne pepper
pinch of nutmeg

Mix together the ricotta, spinach, cheese, bread crumbs, and seasonings. Add more bread crumbs if necessary to keep mixture firm. Set aside.

2	**PREPARE**	Lightly grease 2 serving plates or bamboo trays on which to steam satchels; or, if using tiered bamboo steamer, then lightly grease racks. Place steaming rack in wok and add water for steaming. Bring water to a boil with rack already in place if using plates.
3	**TRIM** *30 to 40 wonton wrappers*	Place wrappers in stacks of 6 and trim corners off. Round off the squares as much as possible.
4	**FILL**	Place a teaspoonful of filling in the middle of a wrapper. Bring up the edges as if you were wrapping a flowerpot. Make a circle with your thumb and forefinger and squeeze the middle of the satchel; it should have a slight hourglass shape. Filling will blossom to the top. Flatten top by smoothing with the back of a clean spoon dipped in water. Press pasta satchel onto the plate or steamer; bottom will flatten and package will stand on its own. Continue to make satchels until plate is filled. You will have about 35 satchels.
5	**STEAM**	Steam 1 plate or tray over boiling water for 10 to 15 minutes. As soon as the plate or tray is done, steam the next plate. The tiered bamboo racks may be stacked and steamed together.
6	**SERVE**	Lift the plates, tray, or bamboo steamer onto another larger serving plate and serve hot. You can also allow these to cool and reheat with 2 to 3 minutes of additional steaming.

Improvisation not recommended; use all measurements as given.

Spring Rolls

Eggrolls are American, however spring rolls are the authentic Chinese food from which they come. Small and thin, these spring rolls are flaky pastries surrounding a savory and airy-textured filling. You can buy spring roll pastry (see Ingredients), but mostly it is frozen and tends to be tough and too large. I prefer to use filo dough, which produces a dainty and light roll. No buttering is necessary. Instead, during the deep-frying, the hot oil penetrates the layers of dough, separating them and making them light and flaky.

The color of cooked spring rolls is a light gold; they should not be brown. Use a deep-frying thermometer and keep the oil between 300 and 325 degrees. Take the rolls out before they turn thoroughly golden, then re-fry them in batches of four to six each just before serving. That way you can re-heat a great many in a short time, and they will all be hot when you serve them. In fact, the pastry becomes lighter and richer with the double frying. You could even make and fry them a day in advance.

It is still true that a spring roll is only as good as its filling, usually a stir-fry of pork, cabbage, mushrooms, and bean sprouts. Sliver each ingredient finely to retain lightness and balance; the pork, cabbage, and mushrooms should be cut to the size of the bean sprouts. Several recipes are given for cooked fillings, followed by two recipes for fillings which need no cooking.

SERVES 10 AS A FIRST COURSE, 20 AS AN HORS D'OEUVRE

---

1 **WASH**
2 cups bean sprouts

Place the sprouts into a sinkful of water. Swish around. Discard hulls and tails that float to the top. Drain.

---

2 **SOAK**
3 dried black mushrooms

Put mushrooms into a small bowl of water. Soak until swollen, about 30 minutes. When mushrooms are soft, cut off stems and shred caps.

---

3 **CUT AND SEASON**
1/4 pound napa cabbage
1/4 pound boneless pork
1 tablespoon light soy sauce
1 1/2 teaspoons sherry

Shred cabbage. Cut pork into thin slices, then stack 3 to 4 slices and cut into fine shreds. Pour soy sauce and sherry over, and mix.

---

4 **STIR-FRY**
1 tablespoon oil

Pour 1 tablespoon oil into wok set over high heat. Toss the mushrooms in the oil until their aroma wafts up to you. Add the pork and toss at a steady pace. Scoop out meat and mushrooms. Clean wok.

5   **STIR-FRY**
    2 tablespoons oil
    ½ teaspoon salt
	Add oil to wok and then add the cabbage, tossing quickly. Add the bean sprouts and salt, and toss until the cabbage is wilted. Return the pork mixture to wok. Turn the mixture to combine thoroughly, then scoop out and let cool.

6   **ASSEMBLE**
    about 8 sheets filo
      dough, or about
      15 spring roll
      wrappers
    1 egg, beaten
	If using filo dough, thaw according to directions on package. Take scissors and cut through 4 to 5 thicknesses into 5-inch squares. With a fork, pierce through dough, riddling with holes. Do not punch holes in spring roll pastry. Use 2 layers of filo dough or 1 of spring roll dough per spring roll. Place on a work surface with 1 corner pointing at you. Near the bottom corner, place 1 tablespoon of filling for filo dough or 2 tablespoons for spring roll pastry. Pull filling into a long strip with your fingers and lap the bottom edge of pastry over the filling. Paint a ½-inch perimeter of beaten egg on the pastry sheet, then fold the 2 sides over the lapped edge butcher-wrap style. Loosely roll the rest of the dough into a cylinder and place roll on tray or platter. Continue to make remaining rolls. Do not overstuff rolls or they will be dense.

7 **DEEP-FRY** *4 cups oil*	Heat oil to 325 degrees. Slide 3 to 4 rolls into oil and fry, turning once. Remove and drain as soon as they turn blond. Continue to fry remaining rolls.
8 **SERVE**	Serve immediately. If desired, cut each in half and offer light soy sauce, rice vinegar, or Banh Trang sauce (page 102) as a dip.

Spring Rolls with Duxelles and Bean Sprouts

 Although neither this nor the following recipe is traditional, both make very elegant appetizers indeed. After rolling, follow directions on page 67 for deep-frying.

SERVES 10 AS A FIRST COURSE, 20 AS AN HORS D'OEUVRE

1 **WASH**
2 cups bean sprouts

See Spring Rolls, preceding page.

2 **CUT**
*½ pound fresh
    mushrooms
1 small onion*

Slice mushrooms. Cut onion lengthwise into thin strips.

3 **STIR-FRY**
*½ cup butter
½ teaspoon salt*

Melt butter in wok over high heat. Allow foam to die down, then add onion and toss until wilted. Add mushrooms and toss at a leisurely pace for 5 minutes. Add the sprouts and turn the mixture until they have wilted and absorbed flavor but are not soft. Scoop out and let cool. Filling is ready for making spring rolls.

Spring Rolls with a Julienne Mirepoix

 After rolling these, follow directions on page 67 for deep-frying.

SERVES 10 AS A FIRST COURSE, 20 AS AN HORS D'OEUVRE

1	**WASH** *2 cups bean sprouts*	See Spring Rolls, page 66.
2	**CUT** *½ small carrot* *½ stalk celery* *1 small onion* *2 slices boiled ham*	Slice carrot diagonally; stack slices and cut into sticks; you should have about ¼ cup. Peel fibers off celery stalk and slice thinly with the knife at an angle to the stalk; you should have about ¼ cup. Cut onion lengthwise into small strips. Cut ham into slivers.
3	**STIR-FRY** *½ cup butter* *½ teaspoon salt*	Melt butter in wok over high heat. When the foam dies down, stir-fry the onion, carrot, and celery until wilted. Add ham and toss to mix in evenly. Add the bean sprouts and stir-fry until wilted but still crisp. Scoop out and let cool. Form spring rolls.

Quick Spring Rolls

 Spring rolls are a labor-intensive preparation, not always possible with today's life-styles. But by buying the best ingredients and using intelligent techniques, the preparation time may be reduced. The following two recipes circumvent the cutting and then cooking of the fillings, so that you can lavish attention on wrapping the rolls. After rolling, follow directions on page 67 for deep-frying.

ZUCCHINI-CHEESE FILLING

---

1   **GRATE**
1 pound zucchini,
    preferably small
    and tender ones
1 teaspoon salt

Scrub and wash squash. Grate (use food processor if you have one), and put in a bowl. Toss with salt and let stand; the salt will draw out liquid in about 30 minutes. When you can see liquid around the zucchini, pick it up by the fistful and squeeze out liquid.

---

2   **GRATE AND MIX**
¼ pound
    mozzarella
⅛ pound parmesan
    cheese
2 tablespoons
    chopped fresh
    Italian parsley
black pepper
cayenne

Grate cheeses and add zucchini. Mix with seasonings. Fill spring rolls.

MUSHROOM-BEAN SPROUT FILLING

---

1   **SLICE AND SOAK**
½ pound fresh
    mushrooms
2 cups bean sprouts
1 teaspoon salt
pinch of tarragon
pinch of mace

Wipe mushrooms clean and slice thin. Wash bean sprouts as described on page 66. Place mushrooms and sprouts in separate bowls and toss each with ½ teaspoon salt. After about 30 minutes, you will see juices seeping around the vegetables. Pick up with your hands and squeeze out the liquid. Combine the mushrooms and sprouts with tarragon and mace in a heatproof bowl.

---

2   **MELT**
½ cup butter

In a small saucepan, heat butter until it turns brown around the edges. Pour the hot butter over the vegetables and stir. Fill spring rolls.

Spareribs Gorgonzola

This dish vanishes when served with drinks. The gorgonzola imparts a mild fragrance and gives a deep character to the taste.

Spareribs are ideal for this preparation, but often butchers will sell what they call "rib tips." These are the trimmings from the racks of spareribs, and they are fine—and much less expensive; though you'll have some smaller, irregular shapes, they are not unattractive.

SERVES 2 AS A FIRST COURSE, UP TO 8 AS AN HORS D'OEUVRE

1 **MARINATE**
1 pound spareribs,
   cut at 1-inch
   intervals
4 ounces gorgonzola
   cheese
1 tablespoon olive
   oil
1 tablespoon light
   soy sauce
2 teaspoons sherry or
   marsala wine

Place ribs in a bowl. Mix remaining ingredients and mash cheese well. Pour over ribs and leave for 1 to 3 hours. Drain.

2 **DEEP-FRY**
2 cups oil

Heat oil in wok until 350 degrees. Gently slide in one third of the ribs and stir around with the perforated ladle. When the surface of the ribs looks bumpy and begins to brown, remove from wok with ladle and drain on paper towels. Fry remaining ribs in 2 installments.

3 **SERVE**

Serve immediately, as either an hors d'oeuvre or first course.

Stuffed Chicken Wings

The middle section of a chicken wing is often neglected and little appreciated, yet the meat is especially tender. In this recipe the bones are taken out, the space stuffed with a spicy Thai-influenced meat mixture, and then breaded and fried. The skin is roomy and strong and, when stuffed, becomes like a balloon. The wing tip may be left on to serve as a handle. It's a pleasurable and delightful fingerfood indeed.

Note: *The time-consuming task of boning may be done in advance. Don't be intimidated; 30 minutes with a sharp knife will take care of it.*

SERVES 2 TO 3 PEOPLE AS AN APPETIZER

---

1 **BONE**
6 to 7 chicken wings
(about 1 pound)

Cut off drumstick sections and set aside. Into the middle joint, insert the point of a sharp, narrow knife through the skin and between the 2 bones. Cut through the top layer of skin and bring the knife up toward the end of the joint. Cut through the ligaments to separate the 2 bones. Scrape and push the flesh off each bone, twisting the bone off at the wing-tip joint.

---

2 **STUFF**
3/4 pound boneless
  pork, preferably
  Boston butt; or
  ground pork
1 cup water
  chestnuts
2 cloves garlic
2 teaspoons chopped
  coriander leaves
1/2 teaspoon salt

Mince or grind pork. Finely dice water chestnuts and garlic. Mix with remaining ingredients. Using fingers, stuff the wing cavities with this mixture, making a small, plump balloon. (At this point, the wings may be refrigerated for several hours. If they are steamed first, they may be refrigerated for 1 to 2 days or kept frozen.)

---

3 **ASSEMBLE**
1 egg
1 cup bread crumbs

Beat the egg. Spread bread crumbs on a plate close to the stove.

---

4 **DEEP-FRY**
2 cups oil

Heat oil in wok until 350 degrees. Dip each wing into the egg, then into the crumbs. Slide wings into the hot oil—3 at a time. Fry until golden. Lift out and drain on paper towels. Repeat for remaining wings.

---

5 **SERVE**
1 recipe Bahn Trang
  sauce (page 102)

Serve immediately. They may also be fried ahead and reheated in the oven at 350 degrees. Dip wings in sauce.

What do you do with the drumsticks? Braise them as in Butter-glazed Chicken and Onions (page 144) or marinate them in the following mixture, then fry them in the same hot oil as for the Stuffed Chicken Wings, and serve alongside the stuffed wings. The drumsticks must be prepared the night before while the stuffed wings may be prepared on the same day.

MARINATE
¹/₃ cup fish sauce
3 tablespoons sugar
3 tablespoons lime juice
2 tablespoons minced garlic

Pour marinade over the chicken drumsticks and mix well. Refrigerate overnight. Pat dry before deep-frying.

Beef and Basil

The basil for this Thai dish is a small-leaf plant with a slight mauve color in the stems. It is called "holy basil," and may be purchased at Southeast Asian markets. It is used, not as an herb or a garnish, but as a green-leaved vegetable that is stir-fried with the beef. Do not substitute the customary large-leaf basil because its flavor does not quite stand up to beef.

SERVES 4 AS A SMALL COURSE, 2 AS A MAIN DISH

1 **PUREE**
2 hot red peppers, or to taste
4 shallots
4 cloves garlic
1 tablespoon shrimp paste

Seed the peppers and slice them and the shallots. Purée the seasonings in a blender or food processor or pound in a large mortar until you have a paste. If desired, adjust the quantity of hot pepper to your taste.

2 **CUT**
2 cups packed holy basil
8 ounces flank steak

Wash and pinch off individual leaves and leaf clusters, removing them from the central stalk. Discard the stalks. Cut steak across the grain into thin slices, about 1/16 inch thick and to the scale of the basil leaves.

3 **SEASON**
2 teaspoons fish sauce
2 teaspoons sherry

Pour the fish sauce and sherry over the beef slices. Mix thoroughly.

4 **STIR-FRY**
2 tablespoons oil

Heat oil in wok over high heat. Stir-fry the paste first. When heated and the aroma fills the air, add the beef. Toss and stir vigorously. When the meat has lost almost all its redness, add the basil leaves. Toss moderately and then serve immediately, with a great deal of plain rice, especially if you've made the dish spicy.

74

Spring Rolls

PAGE 66

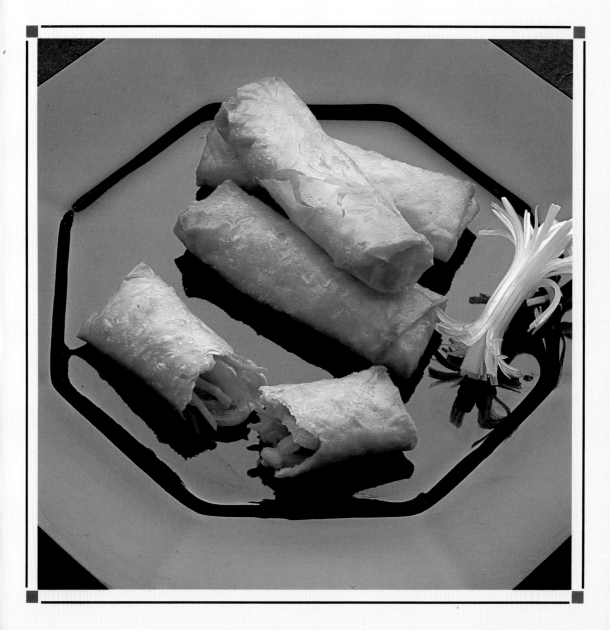

Stuffed Chicken Wings

PAGES 72-73

Savory Garlic Cheesecake

Any filling may go into this basic savory cheesecake but chips of ham or cooked bacon are especially good. Serve a narrow slice for a good first course or a wider slice at a luncheon.

SERVES 4 AS A SMALL COURSE, 6 TO 8 AS AN HORS D'OEUVRE

1 **ROAST AND CHOP**
1 cup garlic cloves, unpeeled

Wrap the garlic in foil and bake in a 400-degree oven until garlic is soft to the touch, about 25 minutes. Peel, then chop roughly.

2 **WHIP**
1 pound cream cheese
1 tablespoon lemon juice
1 teaspoon salt
½ teaspoon pepper
dash of cayenne
pinch each of crumbled bay leaf and sage
½ cup grated parmesan cheese
2 eggs

Beat the cream cheese at high speed in a mixer. Add the seasonings and parmesan cheese, and beat until light and smooth. On medium speed, add eggs 1 at a time, beating just to incorporate.

3 **FOLD**
¼ cup chopped onions
2 tablespoons butter, melted

Place roasted garlic, then onions on top of cheese mixture. Pour very hot butter over the onions, then fold in and blend well.

4 **STEAM**

Bring water to a simmer in wok, with rack in place. Pour the cheese mixture into a buttered 9-inch cake pan or a small loaf pan. Cover with foil. Steam over low heat for 1 hour. Check and replenish with simmering water 2 to 3 times during the cooking. The cheesecake is done when a knife inserted in center comes out clean.

5 **SERVE**
cracker crumbs
spinach leaves

If serving cake warm, let rest for 15 minutes, then turn out. If serving cold, dip pan into hot water first, then turn out. Decorate with cracker crumbs and spinach leaves or more roasted garlic cloves.

Asparagus Timbale

 Poured into a crust, the savory egg custard is a quiche; without the crust, it is a timbale. Here we have a light, Western-style egg custard, or timbale, steamed in Eastern fashion. It contains asparagus spears; and crabmeat or shrimp can also be added to this mixture. *

SERVES 4 AS A SMALL COURSE

---

1 | **CUT AND TRIM** 16 stalks asparagus, preferably slender and young | Snap off the fibrous ends; the stalk will bend and break where the tender section begins. Wash and blot dry.

---

2 | **STEAM** | Bring water to a boil in a wok set over high heat and with steaming rack in place. Steam the asparagus over high heat for 5 minutes. Cool immediately with running water.

---

3 | **STIR** 2 eggs 1¾ cups cream; or 1 cup cream and ¾ cup buttermilk salt and pepper ½ cup grated gruyère cheese dash of cayenne pinch of mace | In a shallow steaming dish, stir the eggs until they are thoroughly blended; do not beat vigorously lest air bubbles coarsen the texture of the custard. Add remaining ingredients. The custard should not be deeper than 1½ inches in its steaming dish.

---

4 | **STEAM** | Turn heat under wok to low and place custard dish on rack. Steam for 15 to 20 minutes. When custard is almost set, arrange the asparagus spears on top in an attractive design. If using shrimp, also add now. If adding crabmeat, scatter over top and then press down into custard gently. Cover and steam until set, about 5 to 10 minutes more, depending on the depth of the custard. A tester should come out clean.

---

5 | **SERVE** 2 tablespoons unsalted butter, sliced thin | Lift the timbale out of steamer and place on platter. Pour off liquid at the top; this liquid is a result of the condensed water coming off the lid. Dot with butter slices and serve immediately by spooning out servings.

**Improvisation not recommended; use all measurements as given.*

Timbale Chinoise

This is a substantial Asian-style custard with minced pork. Instead of a cream or milk base, it uses stock.*

1	**MIX** *2 eggs* *³⁄₄ cup ground pork, preferably hand minced or run through food processor* *1 teaspoon salt or light soy sauce* *¹⁄₈ teaspoon sugar* *1¹⁄₂ cups chicken stock*	Stir eggs in steaming dish. Do not beat them; you'll get a smoother custard by stirring. Add pork and salt. Stir stock into the eggs and be certain that custard is no deeper than 1½ inches in the dish.
2	**CLEAN AND SEASON** *¹⁄₄ cup small shrimp* *pinch of salt or dash of light soy sauce* *1 teaspoon sherry*	Peel and devein the shrimp. Mix with seasonings.
3	**STEAM**	Bring water to a simmer in wok with rack in place. Steam custard over low heat for 10 minutes. When custard has almost set, arrange shrimp in a design over top. Re-cover and steam until custard is done and shrimp turn pink.
4	**SERVE** *minced scallions*	Lift steaming dish out onto a platter. Pour off the layer of water that has collected over top of custard. (This is the condensed moisture from the dome of the steamer.) Sprinkle with scallions and serve by spooning portions out onto individual plates.

*Improvisation not recommended; use all measurements as given.

Shrimp Soufflé Surprises

These are airy balls of shrimp purée, lightened with beaten egg whites and flecks of butter. It seems much more appropriate to use the French name, Boules de Soufflé aux Crevettes!

SERVES 4 AS A SMALL COURSE, 8 AS AN APPETIZER

---

1 **SLICE AND FREEZE**
¼ *pound pork fat or butter*

Partly freeze the fat to firm it—it will slice easier—or have the butcher pre-slice it for you by machine. Cut into the thinnest of slices, about ¾ inch long. Re-freeze briefly, separated, on a tray.

---

2 **PUREE**
1 pound peeled and deveined shrimp
2 teaspoons ice water

Place shrimp in a food processor or blender and purée. Add the ice water a little at a time to get a smooth mixture. Add partly frozen fat to the shrimp in the processor. Spin quickly; you should have small flecks of fat in the smooth shrimp paste. Refrigerate.

---

3 **MIX**
1 scallion
1 slice gingerroot
2 teaspoons sherry
1 teaspoon salt

Crush the scallion and ginger under the blade of a knife. Swirl and swish them in the sherry, then discard. Add seasoned sherry to the shrimp paste, along with salt.

---

4 **BEAT AND FOLD**
4 egg whites

Beat whites until stiff. Fold into shrimp purée.

---

5 **DEEP-FRY**
2 cups oil

Heat oil for deep-frying until 325° degrees. Drop shrimp mixture into hot oil in tablespoonfuls, adding no more than 4 spoonfuls at a time to the wok. They are done within seconds. Remove as soon as they are tanned, not browned.

---

6 **SERVE**

Serve immediately, best when very hot. Accompany with roasted salt (page 181), or offer plain.

Miso Omelette

Omelettes, frittatas, fuyungs—these are gastronomical siblings, and all can be made easily in a wok. Miso—Japanese fermented soy bean paste—is folded into the eggs and this combination of creamy egg and savory miso results in a startling flavor reminiscent of an aged, warm gruyère.

SERVES 2 TO 4 AS A SMALL COURSE

1 **BEAT**
6 eggs
2 tablespoons water
1 teaspoon oil or
    melted butter

Place ingredients in a bowl and whip with a whisk.

2 **HEAT**
3 tablespoons oil or
    butter
2 tablespoons miso
    mixed with 2
    teaspoons water

Add oil to the wok placed over high heat. Swirl oil up the sides, then pour the egg mixture in. Swirl until you have an 8- to 10-inch circle of egg. When egg is partially set, place the miso in the middle. Spread it into a long strip, then fold the omelette into thirds. Lift the omelette onto a plate and place seam side down. Serve immediately.

Stuffed Acorn Squash

This is a simple dish, uncluttered and light on the palate but also subtle. To eat, remove the pork filling and scrape the squash onto a plate. Spoon the gravy over it and accompany with rice or noodles.

SERVES 4 AS A FIRST COURSE

---

1 **CUT AND SCORE**
2 small acorn squash
½ teaspoon salt

Halve the squash and scoop out seeds. Score the flesh with ½-inch checks. Rub scored sections with salt. Cut off a thin slice from the bottom so it can stand stable.

---

2 **MINCE AND SEASON**
1 pound boneless pork, preferably Boston butt; or 1 pound ground pork
1 spoke of whole star anise
pinch of cinnamon
pinch of nutmeg
2 tablespoons light soy sauce
2 teaspoons sherry

The meat is sweeter if you mince it by hand; or cut into small pieces and place in a food processor to mince. You don't want a paste. Set mixture into a mixing bowl. Split the pod of anise and discard the seed, then grind the pod. Mix into the pork along with the cinnamon, nutmeg, soy sauce, and sherry.

---

3 **ASSEMBLE**
4 teaspoons honey

Pat the squash dry. Coat the flesh with honey, then mound the pork mixture into the hollows. Place on a steaming plate.

---

4 **STEAM**

Bring water to a boil in wok, with rack in place. Steam squash over medium high heat for 35 to 45 minutes. Check intermittently to refill wok with water and add boiling water when necessary. After 35 minutes, pierce squash with a fork. If it slides in deep and easily, it is done.

---

5 **MIX**
2 teaspoons light soy sauce
1 tablespoon honey

Pour off liquid collected in steaming plate. Flavor it with the soy sauce and honey and drizzle over squash.

Feta Cheese Stir-fried Spinach

With two ingredients that recall Greek flavors, this recipe takes place in the speedy wok. Choose your spinach discriminatingly. Buy more than the recipe indicates so you can pick through for the best pieces. When sold in bunches, with the roots left on, it is fresher and sweeter than the packaged. I prefer the variety with the pointed, not curly, leaves; it has a rosy blush near the base of the stem.

SERVES 2 AS A SMALL COURSE, 4 AS A SIDE DISH

1 **WASH AND TRIM**
2 bunches fresh
  spinach, about 1
  pound

Choose tender, small-leaved spinach. Wash thoroughly to rid of dirt. (Don't discard the stems if you have young greens; they are crisp, juicy, and succulent.) Place spinach in a colander and stamp the colander smartly against the sink to fling off excess moisture.

2 **STIR-FRY**
3 tablespoons oil
1 clove garlic, lightly
  crushed
1 shallot, lightly
  crushed

Heat oil in wok and render the garlic and shallot. Discard when they begin to brown. Pour in the spinach all at once and toss vigorously. Once the leaves come in contact with the hot oil, they will wilt and shrink in volume.

3 **STEAM**
3 tablespoons feta
  cheese

Add the feta, crumbling it in. Toss quickly, then cover for 30 seconds. The water on the leaves will steam the spinach. Lift cover. The cheese should be softened but not thoroughly melted.

4 **SERVE**
salt to taste

Taste spinach mixture. Add salt if necessary. Serve immediately as a small course or as an accompaniment to other dishes.

Provençale Peppers

For a short time in the summer, markets have a glorious assortment of sweet and hot peppers in delicate tints of yellow, muted greens, and shades of red. My favorites are the banana peppers with their not-too-thick flesh or skin. The following recipe is for banana peppers, which I like hot. You may also use other small peppers, hot or sweet. For a winter variation, use the available thick-fleshed bell peppers.

SERVES 4 AS A FIRST COURSE

---

1 | **CUT AND SEED**
1 *pound banana*
peppers | Trim and halve each pepper lengthwise and take out the seeds. Rinse and dry thoroughly by patting with a towel, then lay them out on a towel for at least 10 minutes to dry.

---

2 | **DRY-FRY**
½ *teaspoon salt*
½ *teaspoon pepper*
¼ *teaspoon each*
dried thyme,
rosemary, savory,
marjoram
1 *teaspoon dried*
parsley | Heat the wok until very hot but do *not* add oil. Pour in the salt, pepper, and dried herbs. (Ideally, you should use dried herbs on the stem, but these are difficult to find; if you have them, use about 1 tablespoon each of stemmed herbs for the ¼ measures indicated.) Toss until fragrances are released and salt turns brown.

---

3 | **STIR-FRY** | Pour peppers into the salt and herb mixture. Use spatula to flatten and press pieces against the wall of the wok so they singe. Continue with this mashing until each piece has mottled brown streaks on its skin.

---

4 | **ADD**
¼ *cup olive oil*
1 *clove garlic*
1½ *tablespoons red*
wine vinegar | Pour oil down the sides of the wok and toss the peppers at a vigorous pace. Press the garlic onto the peppers, then add the vinegar. Continue to stir-fry over high heat until vinegar is evaporated.

---

5 | **SEASON**
1 *tablespoon fish*
sauce
1½ *tablespoons*
sugar (optional)
¼ *teaspoon cayenne*
(optional) | If desired, add fish sauce. Add sugar if the peppers are sharp and stingingly hot. If you have used sweet peppers only, add the cayenne. Remove peppers from wok and serve warm or cold.

Carrot Roux

This is a purée of carrots that is slowly turned with butter in the wok. As the butter cooks, it releases a nutty aroma; any excess liquid evaporates and the purée toasts in the browned butter. This mixture will have more body than a purée—not as soft as baby food—and it is good as a course in itself, although it is more normally a side dish. Serve it plain or shape a nest of it and fill it with toasted pinenuts, steamed tiny green peas, or steamed bay scallops.

SERVES 2 AS A SIDE DISH

1 | **COOK**
2 cups peeled and sliced carrots | Place carrots in a saucepan with water almost to cover. Bring to a boil, then cook over medium heat until just tender. Drain. Put through a food mill until you have a purée.

2 | **STIR-FRY**
¼ cup unsalted butter
1 clove garlic, bruised | Melt butter in wok over medium heat until it browns around the edges. Add the garlic. Pour in the purée and turn the mixture to incorporate into butter. Turn up heat, and continue to turn the purée until it thickens.

3 | **SEASON**
½ teaspoon sugar (optional)
salt to taste | Taste the purée. Remove the garlic. If the carrots were not very fresh, you may need to add sugar. Season very sparingly with salt and serve hot.

Fried Okra

When okra is picked fresh and small—no longer than a thumb—it is very good. Fried with a dusting of flour or cornmeal, it is a simple way to show its charms. Here the okra are left whole, to be served as finger food.

SERVES 2 TO 4 AS AN HORS D'OEUVRE

1 **STEAM**
½ pound fresh okra

Pierce each okra with a fork. Steam in wok over high heat for 3 minutes. Let cool. (This may be done hours in advance.)

2 **HEAT**
2 cups oil

Place oil in wok and heat for deep-frying to 350 degrees.

3 **COAT**
2 tablespoons flour
salt and pepper

Combine flour with salt and pepper. Lightly dust the steamed okra. Shake off excess flour.

4 **DEEP-FRY**

Slide okra into the hot oil and fry in 2 batches. Nudge the mass in a leisurely manner with the perforated ladle. Remove and drain on paper towels.

5 **SERVE**
hot sauce, such as
Sirija (page 35)

Offer hot sauce or mayonnaise flavored with a trace of Worcestershire sauce to dip okra in.

Bean Sprouts Stir-fried with Green Peppers

 A clean, crisp combination with a light texture. Both vegetables are sweet and release compelling aromas when cooked in oil. Take care to cut the pepper to the size of the sprouts, or the two will not mix evenly and the texture will be lost.

SERVES 2 AS A SIDE DISH

1	**WASH** *1/2 pound bean sprouts*	Swirl the sprouts in a sinkful of water. The hulls and root tails will rise to the surface. Discard these and dredge out the sprouts. Place in a colander to drain.
2	**CUT** *1 green bell pepper* *2 scallions*	Cut pepper into thin strips, along the grain, to match the size of the sprouts. You could also use a food processor to shred the pepper. Cut the white sections of the scallions into 1½-inch segments. Quarter each section lengthwise. Set green parts aside for another purpose.
3	**STIR-FRY** *1 tablespoon oil*	Heat oil in wok over high heat. When oil is hot, toss in the green pepper and stir-fry until the aroma wafts up, about 1 minute. Scoop out. Wipe wok clean.
4	**STIR-FRY** *2 tablespoons oil* *salt to taste*	Heat oil in wok over high heat. When hot, add scallions. As they wilt, add sprouts and toss at a steady pace for 2 minutes. Add salt and toss, then put in green pepper. Toss to combine, then serve immediately.

NOTE: If you have a quantity of chives, stir-fry them with sprouts. Use the lower, root end of the chives by harvesting them below ground level. The tops don't have much flavor and when wilted can be grassy tasting. Cut the lower third of the chives into 2-inch lengths to match the sprouts. You'll need 3 cups of chives to 1/2 pound of sprouts, then proceed with recipe as given above, adding chives during the last 15 seconds of tossing.

Ratatouille in a Wok

This is a favorite that takes advantage of summer harvests. The separate frying of each vegetable is easy to do in the wok. I recommend the slender, small eggplants commonly referred to as "oriental."

SERVES 4 TO 8 AS A SIDE DISH

1 **CUT AND DRAIN**
½ *pound eggplants*
1 *teaspoon salt*

Peel and cut eggplants into ½-inch-thick rounds. Then cut the rounds into sticks. Toss the eggplant pieces with the salt and leave to drain in a colander. Pat dry and set aside.

2 **CUT**
2 *medium onions*
½ *pound zucchini*
1 *bell pepper*
4 *medium tomatoes, peeled and seeded; or 1 can (23 ounces) tomatoes, drained*
2 *cloves garlic, peeled*

Cut onions into eighths. Scrub the zucchini and cut into sticks the size of the eggplant sticks. Seed and cut pepper to same size. Squeeze seeds from tomatoes, then cut into ½-inch-wide wedges. Mince garlic finely.

3 **STIR-FRY**
5 *tablespoons olive oil, approximately*

Heat oil in wok, then add eggplant. Fry over high heat until tender, turning mixture patiently as eggplant cooks. Drizzle additional oil down side of wok if eggplant begins to stick and brown. Scoop out when eggplant is tender; the flesh will look opaque and a corner of the spatula should go in and come out as if it were soft butter. Set aside.

4 **STIR-FRY**
4½ *tablespoons olive oil*

Using 1½ tablespoons for each, stir-fry first the zucchini and scoop out. Wipe wok clean, add additional oil, and then stir-fry the pepper; scoop out. Wipe wok clean, then add remaining oil and stir-fry the onions.

5 **COMBINE-COOK**
*salt and pepper to
taste*
pinch of cayenne
*2 tablespoons
minced fresh
parsley*
*1 teaspoon chopped
fresh mint leaves*
*½ teaspoon chopped
fresh basil leaves*
*¼ teaspoon each
dried oregano,
marjoram, and
savory*
*1 cup fresh mint
leaves*

When onions have softened, pour in the reserved eggplant. Toss at a moderate pace until well combined. Add tomatoes and salt, pepper, and cayenne. Turn mixture, cover, and simmer for 3 to 5 minutes. Uncover. If there is excess moisture from tomatoes, boil with cover off to evaporate it. Give mixture a turn intermittently while liquid boils off. Add zucchini and pepper and fold in along with minced garlic, parsley, and dried herbs. Turn off heat and toss in fresh mint leaves.

6 **SERVE**
*additional fresh
herbs*

Serve hot or cold, garnished with additional parsley, basil, or mint.

Snow Pea Greens

You would expect the leaves of the sweetest peas to be every bit as delicious and edible as the pod. They are. Snow pea greens, gathered from the sprouts of the plant when they are very young, are stir-fried with a little wine to make this delectable treat.

If you grow your own snow peas, pinch 6 inches off the tops of the newly sprouted plants. They will come back, don't worry—but there is only one short time in the season when you can have this delicacy. The stalk part of the sprout should be tender. Bite into one. If it is tough, pinch off the leaves from the lower stem and keep pinching until you reach the upper stem where it is tender. The leaves can remain attached to the edible stem; discard the lower part.

SERVES 2 TO 4 AS A SMALL COURSE OR SIDE DISH

---

1 | **WASH AND TRIM**
1 to 2 quarts snow
*   pea sprouts* | Wash sprouts in a sinkful of water, trimming as described. You should have a fluffy mass of green leaves. Place in colander and stamp colander smartly several times to fling off excess water.

---

2 | **STIR-FRY**
3 tablespoons oil
1 clove garlic,
*   bruised*
1 shallot, bruised
salt to taste
1 tablespoon sherry | Heat oil in wok over high heat. When oil is hot, add the garlic and shallot and render briefly. Remove when they begin to brown. At once, add the pea leaves and toss vigorously. Coat with hot oil; they will begin to wilt. When the volume of the leaves shrinks considerably, add salt and toss. Add wine, then turn with spatula. Cover and let mixture steam under high heat for 15 seconds. Taste greens. They should be tender but a fresh, deep green. Add additional salt if necessary and serve immediately.

NOTE: Watercress can also be stir-fried this way. Trim off the thick fibrous stalks before stir-frying.

Culled Vegetables

The wok's ample berth is superb for parboiling bulky or voluminous vegetables. Once the water has come to a boil in the wok, you can plunge in corn on the cob, spinach, cauliflower, broccoli, beans, turnips, and greens of all kinds. With a few raking motions of the ladle, the vegetables are thoroughly and evenly cooked and only two or three scoops with the ladle lift out the pieces. You have absolute control; every vegetable is visible and reachable.

This set of recipes is named "culled" because of the deeply satisfying act of gathering the beautiful vegetables from their water bath. Several recipes are given; the sauces are interchangeable.

Culled Spinach with Toasted Almond Butter

In this recipe the spinach remains a fresh, eye-pleasing green and has an interesting texture. The simple toasted almond butter is poured over.

SERVES 4 AS A SIDE DISH

1	**WASH AND TRIM** 2 bunches young spinach, about 1½ pounds	Wash spinach thoroughly in a basin of water, then cut off roots and separate the stems (often very sweet and tender).
2	**TOAST** ¼ cup slivered almonds ¼ cup butter	In a small saucepan or frying pan over high heat, toast the almonds, moving them around steadily. When the almonds are lightly browned and fragrant, add the butter. Set aside.
3	**BOIL** 6 cups water salt to taste	Bring water to a boil over high heat, with lid on. Plunge in the spinach and push and dunk with the perforated ladle. As soon as spinach wilts, remove with just a few swipes of the ladle and place into a serving dish. Press the ladle against the spinach and pour out excess water. Pour the toasted almonds and butter over the greens, toss, season with salt, and serve.

Culled Broccoli with Anchovy and Garlic Sauce

 This sauce is cold and can be made ahead of time. The broccoli need not be culled with the same immediacy as spinach because it does not overcook as readily.

SERVES 4 AS A SIDE DISH

1 | **WASH AND TRIM**
1 bunch broccoli | Wash broccoli and peel stems. Quarter each stem up through the flower lengthwise.

2 | **MIX**
1 clove garlic
1 shallot
½ cup olive oil
1 teaspoon anchovy paste
salt and pepper | Put garlic through a press. Mince shallot. Stir shallot and garlic into the olive oil. Add anchovy paste and salt and pepper to taste. Set aside.

3 | **BOIL**
6 cups water | Bring water to a boil in the wok set over high heat. Place broccoli into the water and cover. Return water to a boil and test. Broccoli should still be a bright green, but be tender and hot all the way through. Remove to a serving dish and pour off excess water. Pour the cold sauce over the hot broccoli, toss, and serve.

French-fried Beans
Provençale

PAGE 94

Warm Beef Salad

PAGE 99

Culled Asparagus with Soy-sesame Sauce

 You don't need an asparagus cooker to fix asparagus.

SERVES 4 AS A SIDE DISH

1 **WASH AND TRIM**
   1 pound asparagus, about ½ inch thick

Buy asparagus that are uniform in size. Snap off the tough and fibrous ends; the stem will give easily at exactly where it is tender.

2 **MIX**
   1 tablespoon soy sauce
   2 tablespoons oil
   1 tablespoon Asian-style sesame oil
   1 teaspoon sugar
   1 teaspoon rice, cider, or wine vinegar

Stir sauce ingredients in a bowl. Set aside.

3 **BOIL**
   4 to 6 cups water

Bring water to a boil in a wok set over high heat. Place the asparagus into the boiling water and cover wok. When the water returns to a boil, test asparagus. It should be heated through and tender, but be a fresh green in color. Remove to a serving dish and drain off residual water. Pour the sauce over the asparagus, toss briskly, and serve immediately.

Culled Turnip Greens with Crumbled Bacon Sauce

This is my version of southern turnip greens. They remain fresh and green and slightly crisp in the stem, but you must have very tender and young greens.

SERVES 4 AS A SIDE DISH

---

1 **COOK**
4 slices bacon
1 tablespoon oil

Cook bacon until crisp in a skillet. Drain, then crumble. Leave the bacon fat in the pan, and add the oil. (This may be done well in advance.)

---

2 **WASH AND TRIM**
1 pound tender
  turnip greens

Wash and trim greens, eliminating any tough stems or leaves.

---

3 **BOIL**
6 cups water
salt to taste

Bring water to a boil in wok placed over high heat. Add turnip greens all at once and press with the perforated or wire ladle to submerge them. As soon as they are tender but are still bright green, remove to a serving dish and pour off residual water. Reheat bacon fat and pour the hot fat over the greens, season with salt, and sprinkle the crumbled bacon over. Toss briskly and serve.

French-fried Vegetables

The technique of cooking in a large amount of oil at a very high temperature is a wonderful way to prepare vegetables, especially when fried without a batter coating. After taking such a hot bath, these vegetables can absorb extra flavors of a savory sauce. They have the additional virtue of being able to be served either hot or at room temperature. I have named these vegetable recipes "french-fried" after the potatoes, but each is accompanied by a sauce. The sauces are interchangeable.

French-fried Zucchini with Italian Sauce

SERVES 4 AS A SIDE DISH

1	**CUT** *1½ pounds zucchini, 6 inches long and 1 inch thick*	Scrub zucchini thoroughly with a brush. Cut into 2-inch logs, then split each into 6 sticks. Lay the pieces of zucchini on paper towels and press another towel over them.
2	**DRY**	Leave zucchini for at least 30 minutes to dry.

3	**CUT AND PEEL**
	*2 cloves garlic
	1 medium onion
	4 large tomatoes, or
	    1 can (23 ounces)
	    whole tomatoes*
		Mince garlic. Chop onion. Peel tomatoes and squeeze out seeds; dice.

4	**DEEP-FRY** *4 to 6 cups oil*	Heat oil in wok to 350 degrees. Gently slide zucchini in and cook until zucchini begin to brown. Remove with a perforated ladle and drain. Drain oil from wok.

5	**STIR-FRY**
	*¼ cup olive oil
	1 cup crumbled
	    Italian sausage,
	    hot or sweet*
		Add olive oil to wok set over high heat. Toss the garlic and onion around until soft. Add sausage, break up with the spatula, and stir-fry. When meat turns color, in about 5 minutes, add tomatoes.

6	**SIMMER** *½ cup red wine salt and pepper ¼ teaspoon cayenne*	Add wine and seasonings, then let mixture come to a boil. Cover, turn down heat, and simmer until most of the liquid is absorbed. Serve hot or at room temperature.

French-fried Beans Provençale

SERVES 4 AS A SIDE DISH

1 **WASH AND TRIM**
1 pound tender
young green
beans

Take the tips off the beans but do not snap them. Lay beans on paper towels and press another towel over them to absorb all moisture.

2 **DRY**

Leave beans for at least 30 minutes to dry completely. This is crucial because wet beans will splatter and explode during frying.

3 **CUT**
2 cloves garlic
1 medium onion
1 sweet bell pepper
4 medium tomatoes,
   or 1 can (23
   ounces) peeled
   whole tomatoes

Peel and mince garlic. Dice onion. Dice pepper. Peel, seed, and dice tomatoes.

4 **DEEP-FRY**
4 to 6 cups oil

Add oil to wok and heat to 350 degrees. Have enough oil to almost submerge the beans. And beans and, with the perforated ladle, turn the mass every now and then. Gently press the mass from above to dunk the beans into the oil. When the beans are puffy, somewhat wrinkled, and hint at browning around the edges, lift out with the ladle. Drain on paper towels. Drain oil from wok.

5 **STIR-FRY**
1/3 cup olive oil

Add olive oil to wok and stir-fry garlic and onion over high heat until onion has softened. Then add the pepper and tomatoes.

6　**SEASON**
salt and pepper
¹/₄ teaspoon dried
*　oregano*
¹/₄ teaspoon dried
*　thyme*
1 tablespoon dried
*　parsley; or 2*
*　tablespoons*
*　minced fresh*
¹/₂ teaspoon dried
*　basil*
¹/₃ cup red wine

Add seasonings and wine to wok and bring sauce to a boil. Add beans, cover, and bring mixture to a boil. Turn heat down to medium and cook with lid off until the liquid has evaporated.

7　**SERVE**
fresh parsley or basil

Serve beans hot or at room temperature. If left overnight, the flavors actually intensify; just remove from refrigerator a few hours before serving to allow to come to room temperature. Garnish with parsley or basil.

Fried Beans, Sichuan Style

 This is the traditional Chinese recipe for the style of recipes earlier dubbed "French-fried." The original bean used in this dish is the "yard-long" bean, actually about 16 inches in length; however, regular green beans will serve as well. The one ingredient for which there is no substitute is preserved kohlrabi. It is not pretty. After intensive and prolonged curing, it looks like a gnarled and sinuous brown fist, but it imparts a unique peppery and salty taste to the dish. (See Ingredients, page 37.)

SERVES 4 AS A SIDE DISH

---

1 | **TRIM**
1 pound yard-long beans or green beans | Pinch off tips. If you have yard-longs, snap into 3-inch sections; do not snap regular green beans. Wash thoroughly.

---

2 | **DRY** | Dry beans thoroughly with paper towels, then leave to sit for 30 minutes.

---

3 | **CUT**
a 1-inch slice pickled kohlrabi, approximately
4 scallions
1 to 2 fresh cayenne or jalapeño peppers
2 cloves garlic
1 slice gingerroot, about ⅛ inch thick | Rinse off the kohlrabi; place it in a small bowl with water to cover. Slice the scallions into ¼-inch pieces. Seed the peppers and cut them, the garlic, and the ginger into ⅛- to ¼-inch dice. Then cut the kohlrabi to the same size.

---

4 | **MINCE**
¼ pound boneless pork | Mince meat by hand or in the food processor until very fine. (You can substitute butcher-ground pork, although it is coarser.)

---

5 | **DEEP-FRY**
4 to 6 cups oil | Heat oil in wok until 350 degrees. Slide the beans in and turn and poke them with the spatula at a leisurely pace. They are done when the skin begins to brown and look slightly wrinkled and puffy. Remove with the perforated ladle and allow to cool. When the oil has cooled enough to handle safely, drain most of it off but leave about ⅓ cup in wok for cooking the sauce.

6	**STIR-FRY** *¼ cup oil* *1 teaspoon light soy sauce* *1 tablespoon dark soy sauce* *2 tablespoons Zijiang or cider vinegar* *2 tablespoons brown sugar*	Heat oil in wok over high heat. Toss the garlic, ginger, and scallion pieces until their fragrances reach your nose. Add the kohlrabi. Toss at a leisurely pace for about 2 minutes. Add meat and stir-fry until no longer pink, about 5 minutes. Pour in seasonings, vinegar, and sugar, and mix.
7	**SIMMER** *½ cup water*	Add the fried beans and toss to coat with the sauce. Add the water and bring to a simmer. Cover wok and cook mixture for 5 minutes. Turn the mixture intermittently.
8	**SERVE**	Lift the lid and boil off excess liquid. Serve hot or at room temperature.

French-fried Carrots with Garlic-pickle Sauce

 The taste and smell of the carrots during and after the deep-frying is absolutely seductive. You may have to triple the amount of carrots to fry enough to appease the immediate appetites of your family. Then use the carrots left over to cook in this spicy sauce.*

SERVES 4 AS A SIDE DISH

---

1 **CUT**
1½ to 2 pounds carrots

Don't peel the carrots. Cut into 3-inch sticks about ¼ to ½ inch around. Wash and rinse.

---

2 **DRY**

Allow carrots to dry for 30 minutes.

---

3 **CUT**
4 cloves garlic
6 green onions
¾ cup pickle relish
⅓ cup chopped cayenne or jalapeño peppers, or equivalent in sweet peppers

Mince the garlic. Slice the onions into thin rounds. You will want everything to be about the size of the bits of pickle relish. Mix with peppers and set aside. (If your tongue is not willing, substitute sweet peppers and control the heat in the dish by addition of a little cayenne pepper in small increments when you season the dish.)

---

4 **DEEP-FRY**
4 to 6 cups oil

Heat oil in wok to 350 degrees. Gently slide the carrots into the hot oil. Cook until the carrots just begin to brown. Remove with a perforated ladle and drain. Drain oil from wok and rinse.

---

5 **STIR-FRY**
⅓ cup olive oil

Add olive oil to wok and cook the garlic, onions, and peppers until the aroma reaches you. Add the fried carrots.

---

6 **SEASON AND SIMMER**
1 tablespoon cider vinegar
1 tablespoon brown sugar
1 teaspoon salt
1 cup red wine

Turn heat down and add seasonings. (If substituting sweet pepper, add ¼ teaspoon cayenne and increase to taste.) Add wine and cover. Increase heat and bring to a boil. Reduce to a simmer and cook until the liquid is almost totally absorbed. Serve hot or at room temperature.

---

*Improvisation not recommended; use all measurements as given.

Warm Salads

Although warm salads and stir-fries are similar, several important characteristics distinguish them. The seasoning for a warm salad is vinegar and an aromatic oil. In a stir-fry, the taste comes from salt or soy sauce, and the oil is more neutral because it penetrates the vegetables while they cook, releasing their juices. In a warm salad, the oil coats the ingredients as it would in a cold salad. The meats in a stir-fry are cut raw, then cooked in oil until done whereas in a warm salad, they are pre-cooked and at the time of serving are lightly heated and then sliced with the pan juices poured over. The wok is the perfect utensil for tossing a warm salad.

Warm Beef Salad

This is the first of three warm salads. Leftover roast beef or grilled steak, especially rare portions with natural juices, are the basis for the dish, but you can also make this with a fresh piece of flank steak.

SERVES 2 AS A SMALL COURSE

1 **WASH**
1 bunch watercress
8 leaves curly endive
(chicory)

Trim watercress of tough stems. Trim endive of dark green leafy parts. Wash and drain both.

2 **HEAT**
1/3 cup olive oil
1/2 pound leftover
roast beef or
uncooked flank
steak
1 tablespoon
balsamic or wine
vinegar
salt and pepper
2 teaspoons
Dijon-style
mustard
pinch of ground
coriander

Warm 2 plates in the oven. Heat oil in wok over high heat, then slip in slice of roast beef or flank steak to sear the outsides. Take out, leaving the oil, and place in the oven on one of the plates. Add vinegar to wok, then add all remaining seasonings. Bring to a boil; if you have some leftover roasting juices (about 1 tablespoon), stir it in too. Add watercress and endive and immediately turn off the heat (on an electric stove, move wok to a cool burner). Toss leaves to coat with dressing until they wilt.

3 **SERVE**

Divide salad mixture into the 2 plates and arrange attractively. Quickly slice the meat into thin sheets and lay them over the wilted greens. Spoon hot pan juices over.

Warm Chicken Liver Salad with Asparagus and Greens

 The stems of spinach leaves can be delectable. When young and tender, they are refreshingly sweet. Include them if you have small spinach leaves, but taste them raw first. You will be able to tell if they are too fibrous to use.

SERVES 4 AS A SMALL COURSE

1 TRIM
20 leaves spinach
8 leaves curly endive
20 stalks slender
  asparagus

Wash the spinach; keep whole—leaf connected to the stem—if possible. Trim the endive leaves down to the stem sections; the tips of the leaves tend to be chewy. Break off the root ends of asparagus; the stems will snap naturally where the tender sections begin.

2 STEAM
4 chicken livers

Boil water in wok, with rack in place. Place livers on a small plate and steam them for about 10 minutes or until livers are firm but a little pink in the middle. They will continue to cook while cooling down and when cooled, the juices will not run so red. (The above steps may be prepared ahead of time.)

3 HEAT
½ cup olive oil
1 tablespoon
  balsamic or wine
  vinegar
pinch of five-spice
  powder
salt and pepper

About 10 minutes before serving, warm 4 plates in the oven, then heat the oil in the wok. Toss the livers in the oil. Remove the livers, leaving the oil in the wok, and place on one of the warmed plates. Return to the oven. Pour in the vinegar and scrape the sides of the wok a little to deglaze it. Bring to a boil. Add asparagus, and toss until they are well warmed and the flavor of the vinegar has penetrated to the core—for narrow young asparagus, about 1 minute. Quickly add the leafy vegetables and immediately turn off heat. Toss until the leaves are just wilted. (On an electric stove move the wok to a cold burner.) Add five-spice powder, salt, and pepper to taste.

4 SERVE

Divide and arrange the vegetables on the warmed plates. Quickly slice the livers with a tilted cut and drizzle pan juices over. Serve immediately.

Warm Sprout Salad

In this salad, hot stir-fried sprouts "warm" the cold lettuce.

SERVES 2 AS A SMALL COURSE

1 **WASH**
*1/2 pound bean
    sprouts
12 leaves iceberg
    lettuce*

Rinse the sprouts in a sinkful of water. Skim off excess hulls and root ends which float to the top. Wash the lettuce; pat dry.

2 **TOSS**
*3 tablespoons olive
    oil
2 teaspoons wine
    vinegar
1 clove garlic,
    pressed
salt and pepper to
    taste*

Combine the ingredients for the vinaigrette in a cold wok. Add the lettuce leaves and toss until they are well coated with the dressing. Arrange the leaves in an attractive bed on 2 plates. Leave any traces of vinaigrette in the wok for the next step.

3 **STIR-FRY**
*2 tablespoons oil
1 clove garlic
salt to taste*

Heat oil in wok over high heat and add garlic. Render, then remove when it begins to turn brown. Add the sprouts and toss steadily. When a sweet aroma is released, taste a sprout. It should be hot throughout and not taste raw—about 3 minutes. Arrange sprouts centered over lettuce leaves and serve immediately.

NOTE: *I specify iceberg lettuce because of the icy juiciness of the sprouts and lettuce next to each other, one hot and one cold. Belgian endive and Boston lettuce are also excellent here, however.*

Wrap-up Foods

An absorbing involvement and childlike joy blossom when you allow your guests to put together their own foods. It is entertaining, and it makes for good entertaining. I think it no accident that every cuisine has its wrap-up foods: tacos and moo-shu pork are just the popular examples. Even sandwiches, when offered as superb and multifarious self-fixings, elicit delighted responses.

But when do you serve these dishes? My response is "anytime," whether a cocktail party, buffet, or sit-down dinner. Place them at the opening of the meal to function as an ice-breaker or as the final course to symbolize closure. But they can also be a main meal or a single luncheon, with nothing for you to fix at the last minute.

A word of caution about the serving of these foods. Use small teaspoons, even demitasse spoons, as your utensils. Too often I find my guests trying to stuff their packages, in the style of tacos or hot dog fixings, to overflowing. The food does not taste good in bulk and the seasonings are too strong for voluminous consumption. You will run out of filling, the wrappers will break, and you will find everyone thirsty if large serving spoons are provided.

The following recipes are for wrap-up foods in which the wrappings may be purchased. Four are wrapped in lettuce leaves—light, nonstarchy, and crisp. The leaves may be presented as a wreath of green around the filling. Popia is of southern Chinese origin, and the wrappers are the same as for spring rolls.

Banh Trang

This is Vietnamese. Banh trang *is the name for the thin rice paper sheets used to wrap the filling. The French name* galettes de riz *appears on most packages and conveys well the fine, fragile quality of these pastries.*

The sheets are made from water-ground rice flour. They are paper thin and are sold dried, packaged in a sheaf. Available in either round or rectangular shapes, they are pearly white and extremely brittle, but as soon as they come in contact with water, they become soft and chewy. The Vietnamese prize their chewy character, and just quickly pass the dried sheets under running water. I like them more tender, and soak them for a little while in cold water. The soaking also makes it easier to separate the sheets.

SERVES 4 TO 8 AS A SMALL COURSE

1

PREPARE SAUCE
2 cloves garlic
2 hot red peppers
1/2 cup fish sauce
2 tablespoons lime
 juice
3 tablespoons sugar
1/2 cup water

Peel and mince the garlic. Seed the red pepper and slice very thin. Combine with remaining ingredients in a bowl and stir to dissolve sugar. Let mixture sit and steep while you proceed with rest of recipe. (This sauce may be made a day in advance.)

2	**SOAK** *1 package (1 pound)* banh trang *wrappers, 8 inches* *round*	Carefully separate the sheets as best you can. Place sheets in a sink with 2 inches of water. When softened, drain and place on a serving dish. They tend to glue to each other, but don't worry; separating the sheets is part of the work and fun of the guests.
3	**SOAK AND CLEAN** *3 tablespoons tree* *ears*	Soak tree ears in a bowl of cold water until soft, about 15 minutes. When softened, rinse and swirl in several waters to wash out any trapped sand. Squeeze the mass with your fingertips. When you feel a hard lump, tear it out of the mushroom and discard. Chop coarsely.
4	**MINCE** *1 pound boneless* *pork shoulder or* *ground pork* *2 cloves garlic*	Slice meat thinly and quickly mince in food processor or by hand. Mince garlic.
5	**STIR-FRY** *3 tablespoons oil* *2 tablespoons fish* *sauce*	Add oil to the wok over high heat. When oil is hot, add the garlic. Once the aroma is apparent, add the pork and turn the mixture until the meat is no longer red. Add fish sauce and tree ears and toss thoroughly. Scoop out.
6	**SERVE** *½ cup chopped* *roasted or fried* *peanuts (optional)*	Serve with a bowl of sauce on the side. Guests should place a rounded spoonful of the filling on a sheet of rice paper, drizzle the sauce over the filling, sprinkle with peanuts, and roll and wrap the package butcher-style. Then dip roll in sauce and eat with fingers. When the filling is gone, roll plain sheets up in a cylinder and dunk in the sauce. Or you can preroll the *banh trang* and cut into 1½-inch pieces, drizzle with sauce and peanuts, and serve on individual plates as a first course; this is the more standard Vietnamese service.

Popia

This dish is native to the southern provinces of China, notably Fukien (Fujian), but it has been carried to almost every Southeast Asian country. It is a rich stew of meat, seafood, and vegetables, served with a variety of condiments and rolled in a spring roll wrapper. Since the Fukien live close to the water, the condiments are various elements of the sea. I have not included the seaweed, however the crisp-fried anchovies (see page 62) are important; they give a unique taste and crunchiness. The dish is called popia *after its wrapper, meaning "thin pastry," which is also a spring roll wrapper. If spring roll wrappers are not available, use flour tortillas instead; do not use eggroll wrappers.*

SERVES 8 TO 12 AS A FIRST COURSE, 4 AS A MAIN DISH

---

1 **PEEL**
¾ pound small shrimp

Peel and devein shrimp.

---

2 **CUT**
¾ pound boneless pork
¾ pound napa or green cabbage
1 cake pressed bean curd

Cut pork into slivers. Shred the cabbage. Shred the bean curd to the same size as the meat and cabbage.

---

3 **STIR-FRY**
3 tablespoons oil
2 tablespoons soy sauce
1 tablespoon sherry

Add oil to wok and allow to get hot. Render garlic and then discard when brown. Toss in the pork and cook until it is no longer pink. Add the shrimp and turn the mixture to combine. Season the soy sauce and the sherry and then scoop out. Rinse wok.

---

4 **STIR-FRY**
2 tablespoons oil
2 tablespoons soy sauce

Heat oil in wok over high heat and then add bean curd; toss at a steady pace until aromatic. Add soy sauce and then put pork mixture back in. Turn to combine. Add the cabbage and taste and adjust seasonings. Add more soy sauce if not salty enough.

---

5 **STEW**

Cover wok and cook over very low heat for 1 to 1½ hours. The flavors should mingle without additional liquid, but if the mixture threatens to burn add a little chicken stock or water, about 3 to 4 tablespoons at a time. (This filling mixture may be frozen and reheated before serving.)

| 6 | SERVE
*40 spring roll
wrappers
condiments (see
following)* | Serve hot in an earthenware pot or casserole. Put condiments on the table along with a stack of wrappers. Or pre-roll them and cut each roll into 1-inch segments, place on individual plates, and serve as an appetizer. |

POPIA CONDIMENTS

Prepare these ahead of time.

1	DEEP-FRY *4 cups oil 1 cup raw peanuts 1 cup dried anchovies*	Add oil to wok so that you have at least 2 inches of oil. Heat to 325 degrees, then separately fry the peanuts and the anchovies. Drain and cool, then coarsely chop the peanuts. Cool and crumble the anchovies.
2	FRY *2 tablespoons oil 2 eggs*	In a skillet, lightly cover the bottom with oil. Beat the eggs and make a large, thin pancake in skillet. Cook on both sides and remove to cool. When cooled, roll up and cut into slivers.
3	BLANCH *2 cups bean sprouts*	Bring water to a boil in a saucepan and add sprouts, cook for a second, then refresh in cold water. Drain. (Sprouts can also be steamed.)
4	CUT *1 bunch scallions*	Cut scallions into 3-inch segments. Split each lengthwise and soak in ice water for about 1 hour. They will separate and curl up. Drain.
5	HAVE READY *Chinese mustard hoisin sauce hot sauce*	Prepare separate bowls of the sauces, with spoons in each.
6	ASSEMBLE	Present a colorful smorgasbord of condiments grouped around the *popia* filling and stack of wrappers. Assemble rolls as follows: Place 1 wrapper on your plate. Paint it with a strip each of the sauces, using the back of the spoon. Place 2 rounded tablespoonfuls of filling close to one edge. Put on a few strands of scallion and some bean sprouts. Sprinkle about ½ teaspoon of peanuts, some crumbled fish, and egg slivers over that. Roll up, tucking in one end to keep filling from sliding out. Hold vertically and sink teeth in.

Sausage and Oysters in Lettuce Leaves

 This dish was one of my mother's best. Although the ingredients were somewhat esoteric, we children were undeterred and always managed to put away quantities of it.

There is no substitute for Chinese sausage, although I have found canned smoked oysters a more than satisfactory replacement for the original dried oysters. This dish complements drinks well and is the perfect first course to have people bring their drinks to the dining table.

SERVES 4 TO 8 AS A FIRST COURSE

---

1 **SOAK**
6 dried black
  mushrooms

Place mushrooms in a small bowl with cold water and soak while you proceed with rest of recipe.

---

2 **CUT**
3 Chinese sausages
2 cans (3¾ ounces
  each) smoked
  oysters
2 cups water
  chestnuts

Split sausage in half lengthwise. Cut each half into 4 strips, then dice the strips. You should have ⅛- to ¼-inch dice. Drain the canned oysters by inverting the cans onto a cutting surface. Cut the entire rectangle of oysters into ⅛- to ¼-inch dice. Drain and cut water chestnuts into the same size as sausages and oysters. Drain mushrooms and cut off and discard stems. Cut caps to the same size as other ingredients.

---

3 **STIR-FRY**
3 tablespoons oil
2 tablespoons soy
  sauce,
  approximately

Pour oil into wok set over high heat. When oil is hot, add the sausage and mushrooms. Toss at a moderate pace until the fragrance of the sausage is apparent. Add the oysters and turn the mixture to combine. Finally add the water chestnuts. Add soy sauce and toss thoroughly. Taste; add more soy sauce if not salty enough. (This may be made in advance and served at room temperature.)

---

4 **SERVE**
2 heads Boston
  lettuce

Cut the stems and cores from the lettuces. Wash and separate the leaves, keeping them whole. Trim the bigger, outer leaves to a small size; the leaves should be smaller than the palm of your hand. Arrange around a large platter or tray, and place the oyster mix in the center or in a separate serving bowl. Put 2 to 3 serving teaspoons in the mixture, and show your guests how to scoop 1 rounded teaspoon—not too much—into a curve of lettuce leaf, close the leaf, and bite into it.

Thai Tartare

PAGE 108

Pepperoni Fried Rice

PAGE 116

Egg Fuyung with Crabmeat

In this recipe, the traditional crabmeat omelette is wrapped in lettuce leaves. Bean threads are added for additional texture; they give a smoothness and a body to the omelette.

SERVES 4 TO 6 AS A FIRST COURSE

---

1 **WASH**
1 head Boston lettuce

Trim leaves so none is bigger than the palm of your hand. Wash and pat dry.

---

2 **SOAK**
½ cup bean threads

Place bean threads in a bowl with cold water and soak until softened, about 30 minutes. Snip into 1-inch segments with a scissors.

---

3 **CUT**
1 scallion

Cut into 1-inch sections. Split lengthwise and shred.

---

4 **BEAT**
5 eggs
1 teaspoon salt
½ cup chicken stock

Lightly beat eggs with salt and stock. Set aside.

---

5 **STIR-FRY**
½ cup oil
1 cup shredded crabmeat
1 tablespoon light soy sauce

Add 6 tablespoons oil to wok but do not allow to get too hot. Add the scallion, bean threads, and crabmeat. Toss well and then splash in soy sauce and turn the mixture. Drizzle remaining oil around the edge of the wok, letting it run down into the mixture. Pour in the eggs and allow bottom to set. Flip mixture gently as you would a pancake; don't worry if it breaks and leaks—simply scramble the whole.

---

6 **SERVE**

Serve immediately, with lettuce leaf wrappers on the side or around the omelette. One rounded tablespoon of egg mixture should be wrapped in each leaf.

Thai Tartare

Cool, fresh mint leaves are tossed with raw, or almost raw, beef—a version of the Thai dish lahp. The seasoning is frankly lime, combined with the omnipresent Thai fish sauce and fiery red pepper. I think of this as an Asian version of Steak Tartare.

SERVES 6 TO 8 AS A SMALL COURSE

---

1 **DRY-FRY**
½ *cup white rice*

In a dry wok set over medium heat, toss the rice until toasty brown. Remove and cool. When cooled, crush in a mortar or put through the food processor or blender until a coarse powder.

---

2 **TRIM**
1 cup mint leaves
2 heads Boston or bibb lettuce

Wash and pick through mint leaves. Drain. Cut stem and core from the lettuce, then separate leaves. Trim the large leaves to a 4-inch diameter.

---

3 **MINCE**
1½ pounds lean beef round (not ground)

Slice meat thin, then chop until fine (a cleaver makes this fast work) or put through a food processor.

---

4 **SEASON**
1 clove garlic
2 hot red peppers
¼ *cup fish sauce*
⅓ *cup lime juice*

Put garlic through a press. Seed and finely mince the red pepper. Mix remaining ingredients and add to the beef. Add mint and toss well. Sprinkle with the toasted rice crumbs.

---

5 **SERVE**

Line a platter with lettuce leaves and place beef mixture in center. Diners are to take a teaspoonful of filling and wrap in lettuce leaf.

Family Food

The recipes in this chapter are the meals-in-one, where starch, vegetable, and meat are quickly stir-fried together. They are the hearty dishes—those with robust flavors and self-contained gravies—that save money while emphasizing nutrition. They are the casual meals, for which an accompanying loaf of bread, a tossed salad, or some stir-fried greens are the perfect partners. They are the time-saving recipes, simply and quickly accomplished; and they are the old-time favorites, like lasagna, cannelloni, or stroganoff, so easily done in a wok.

This chapter emphasizes the home techniques of wok cookery: stir-frying, steaming, and braising. If you have gained a good sense of the freedom and quality of cooking in a wok, you will find this grouping of recipes easy and fun. Flexibility and efficiency are important in family cooking, and the wok—and particularly stir-frying—gives a full range of options in that situation. Fried rice and lo-mein, for example, simply add one more step to a basic meat and vegetable stir-fry. Feel free to *ad lib* a little, and double or triple a recipe based on the appetites and size of your family.

Vegetable Rice Ragout

Onions, carrots, peppers, and broccoli are first stir-fried, then cooked with rice for a quick and colorful vegetarian meal.

SERVES 2 PEOPLE

---

1 **CUT**
1 medium onion
2 carrots
1 stalk broccoli
1 bell pepper

Peel the onion, carrots, and broccoli stem. Core the pepper. Cut the onion and pepper into eighths. Slice the carrots and broccoli stem diagonally into pieces ⅛ inch thick. Halve the remaining flowerets (about 2 inches long) lengthwise so that no stem is more than ¼ inch thick.

---

2 **WASH**
1½ cups white rice

Rinse the rice twice in a large saucepan. Set aside.

---

3 **STIR-FRY**
¼ cup oil,
approximately
2 tablespoons soy
sauce

Heat the oil in a wok over high heat. Add the onion and toss at moderate speed until softened, about 3 minutes. Add the pepper and broccoli stem. Toss some more; soon the peppers will be bright green. Add the flowerets and carrots. Add more oil if necessary, then turn the mixture until the broccoli is bright green, another couple of minutes. Stir in the soy sauce and add the rice. Toss to coat rice with oil and to evaporate the water.

---

4 **COOK**
2½ cups water,
approximately

Transfer the mixture to the large suacepan. Pour in the water, using it to rinse rice granules free of the vegetable pieces. Make sure that all the rice grains are submerged in liquid, or else they will not cook. Cover and bring to a boil. Cook over medium-low heat until all liquid has been absorbed, about 10 minutes.

---

5 **SERVE**
grated cheese,
preferably
Parmesan
hot sauce

Serve with additional soy sauce or a sprinkling of cheese and offer hot sauce.

Bok Choy Rice

 Bok choy has become common fare at produce sections of supermarkets. Unfortunately, the commercial variety is often too large and tough for fresh stir-fry treatments, but cut fine and stewed with rice, it makes a tasty dish. The classic Chinese method calls for freshly rendered pork fat to give the rice a fragrant opulence, but this lighter version uses chicken fat. However a cold pressed vegetable oil may be substituted.

SERVES 2 PEOPLE

1	**RENDER** *3 ounces chicken fat*	Heat a clean, dry wok over high heat. Put in the chicken fat, and when you can see a small puddle of melted fat, turn heat to medium. Continue to render until the solid fat is reduced to small bits of cracking floating in the liquid, about 20 minutes. Turn off the heat; remove the cracklings. (This step may be done well in advance.)
2	**WASH** *2 cups white rice*	Rinse the rice 2 times in a saucepan or casserole. Add water to a level ½ inch above the surface of the rice. Bring to a boil over high heat and turn to medium-low to cook.
3	**CUT** *1 pound bok choy*	While the rice is cooking, strip the stalks off bok choy and wash. Reject the really tough outer pieces, then cut tender ones into ½-inch strips. Keep the white stalk sections separate from the leafy parts.
4	**STIR-FRY** *1 slice gingerroot* *1½ teaspoons salt*	Heat the rendered chicken fat (or use 5 tablespoons vegetable oil). Render the ginger and discard. Toss the bok choy stems until they become translucent, about 1 minute, then add the leaves. Toss at moderate pace for 30 seconds. Add salt and incorporate.
5	**COMBINE**	Add bok choy to the half-cooked rice. Give it a few stirs with the spatula, cover, and turn the heat to low. Continue to cook the rice until done—about 10 minutes. When the liquid has been absorbed, stir the rice with a wooden spoon and let it stand uncovered for a minute to evaporate excess steam.

Chicken Rice with 3 Sauces

A magical bond links these two simple but great ingredients; proof of this lies in the existence of a chicken and rice dish in just about every cuisine. This recipe is my secret favorite, a Hainan specialty which remains relatively unknown in this country. The rice is extremely rich since it absorbs the essence of chicken, found best in chicken fat. But don't overcook the chicken; the bone marrow should remain rosey in the center. And although any long-grain rice will work, Jasmine rice is a special treat (see Ingredients). The three dipping sauces follow the recipe and are intended for either dipping a corner of the chicken in the sauce or drizzling over, but are also good whipped into the rice. Or combine all the ingredients from the three sauces into one, for a shortcut.

SERVES 4 PEOPLE

---

1 | **SOAK**
3 cups white rice | Wash rice by sorting through it in a quantity of cold water. Pour off water and repeat. Then add cold water to cover by 1 inch and leave for 1 hour. Drain and leave in a colander.

---

2 | **PREPARE**
1 frying chicken, about 3 pounds | Tear out the pieces of fat just inside the cavity. Let chicken come to room temperature; this can take up to 4 hours out of the refrigerator.

---

3 | **RENDER**
2 to 4 ounces chicken fat | The fat pads removed from a chicken weigh from 1 to 2 ounces. Add enough extra to have a generous 4 ounces, then place fat pieces in a dry wok over high heat. Turn heat down to medium when you see a little liquid rendering out. In 10 to 15 minutes, you will have almost all melted fat (about ⅓ cup) and some little pieces of crackling. Discard or crunch on the cracklings.

---

4 | **STIR-FRY AND COOK**
1 slice gingerroot
½ teaspoon salt
4 cups water, approximately | You should have 6 to 8 tablespoons of fat in wok. If not, add enough vegetable oil to equal that. Heat fat over high heat and add the ginger. When its aroma is released, remove and discard. Add rice and turn grains steadily. When excess water begins to evaporate, the rice will begin to swell and absorb the oil, clinging to each other and making clumps. Add the salt and toss. When all the oil has been absorbed, transfer rice to a straight-sided saucepan. Add water to just skim the surface of the rice by about ⅛ inch. Bring to a boil, cover, and cook on low heat for about 15 minutes.

5 **STEAM**
1/4 teaspoon salt
1 scallion
1 slice gingerroot

Bring water to a boil in wok, with rack in place while rice is cooking. Place chicken in a steaming plate. Rub it inside and out with salt. Insert the scallion and ginger slice into cavity. Place in wok and cover. Steam for 20 minutes, then turn off heat but do not uncover. Leave bird in for another 10 minutes.

6 **SERVE**
1 cucumber

Peel and slice cucumber into pieces 1/4 inch thick. Stir the rice with a wooden spoon, turning the lower layers up. Leave lid off for 2 minutes to let excess steam escape, then transfer to a bowl. When chicken is cool enough to handle, pour out collected liquid and remove ginger slice and scallion from cavity. Cut chicken into quarters or through the bones into several smaller pieces. Place on a serving platter and garnish with cucumber.

SAUCES

SOY DIP
1/4 cup double dark (thick) soy sauce; or 3 1/2 tablespoons dark soy sauce mixed with 1 teaspoon molasses

Place soy sauce in bowl.

GARLIC/PEPPER SAUCE
2 cloves garlic
1 fresh hot red pepper
1 teaspoon vinegar
3 tablespoons water
2 teaspoons sugar

Peel garlic. Seed pepper and cut into 1/4-inch segments. Mash garlic and pepper in a mortar or put through a press using 1 clove at a time along with a few pepper segments. Stir rest of ingredients into the paste.

GINGER SAUCE
2 slices gingerroot
2 scallions (white part only)
3 tablespoons water

Peel ginger and cut into 1/8-inch-thick rounds. Slice scallions. Mash ginger and scallions in a mortar or put through a garlic press, then thin with the water.

Country Club Fried Rice

Fried rice is simple and versatile, but you need to be armed with two basics: a working knowledge of stir-fry techniques; and cold cooked rice, preferably rice which has been cooked without salt and fat because only plain rice will absorb the flavors of the frying process.

Golf clubs in the Far East often have on their menus a fried rice like this one to tantalize their American and European members. Asian children love it as well.

SERVES 2 TO 4 PEOPLE

---

1 | **CUT AND SEASON**
1 medium onion
8 ounces flank steak,
    or round, sirloin,
    or tenderloin tip
2 tablespoons soy
    sauce, preferably
    dark
1 tablespoon sherry | Peel the onion, and cut into 8 sections. Cut the flank steak across the grain into ⅛-inch slices. Pour soy sauce and sherry over the beef and mix.

---

2 | **STIR-FRY**
3 tablespoons oil,
    approximately
4 cups cooked
    plain rice, cold | Heat wok over high heat and add oil. Allow oil to get hot, then add rice. Stir-fry for 3 to 5 minutes, turning often because it tends to stick. Drizzle a little additional oil in a circle down the sides of the wok if you need more. Scoop out the rice and scrape the wok clean.

---

3 | **STIR-FRY**
1½ tablespoons oil | Heat wok over high heat. Pour oil into wok. Heat and add onion. Stir-fry over medium heat until it begins to soften, about 3 to 5 minutes, then scoop out. Wipe wok clean.

---

4 | **STIR-FRY**
1½ tablespoons oil | Heat wok over high heat and add oil. Add garlic and render in the hot oil. Take it out when it browns a little, and add the beef. Toss vigorously for about 30 seconds.

---

5 | **COMBINE-FRY**
1 egg, stirred | As soon as meat has lost most of its red color, add the onion and stir-fry together. Then add the rice, stir, and turn to evenly spread the ingredients and to reheat the rice, about 2 minutes. Pull the rice up the sides of the wok and leave to balance there. You should have a circle of bare wok about 4 inches in diameter. Pour the egg into that spot, letting it partially set, then stir and turn it, exactly as you would scramble an egg. When the scrambled egg is still quite tender and loose, incorporate the rice and turn until ingredients are thoroughly combined.

6 **SERVE**
white or black pepper
hot sauce
cucumber sticks

Remove mixture from wok and serve immediately. Top with a few twists of the pepper mill, and have hot sauce on hand. A few cucumber sticks make a cool and tasty contrast as well as a refreshing garnish.

Jambalaya

In Acadian Louisiana, you will find jambalayas made with everything from guinea hens to oysters to ground beef. Here is one with ham and salt cod.

SERVES 2 PEOPLE

1 **WASH**
2½ cups white rice
¼ cup shredded salt
*   cod*

Rinse and sift through the rice. Drain. Rinse cod and leave in bowl of water to soak and swell, for about 1 hour.

2 **CUT**
1 medium onion
1 stalk celery
2 medium green bell
*   peppers*
¼ pound boiled
*   ham*
4 to 6 cloves garlic

Sliver the onion, celery, green peppers, and ham. Mince the garlic.

3 **STIR-FRY**
¼ cup oil

Heat wok over high heat. Add oil, and when oil is hot, stir-fry the vegetables until wilted, about 5 minutes.

4 **COMBINE-FRY**
¼ cup tomato paste
salt and pepper to
*   taste*
dash of cayenne
2½ cups water,
*   approximately*

Add the ham and salt cod. Toss, then add the rice along with the tomato paste and seasonings. Toss and add the water, being sure there is enough to cover rice. Transfer mixture to a straight-sided saucepan large enough to allow rice to expand. Cook for 15 to 20 minutes, or until rice is done. Serve warm, by itself or as a side dish.

Hamburger Fried Rice

This is the budget version of Country Club Fried Rice. It's a handy family meal.

1 **CUT**
1 medium onion

Peel, and cut into 6 sections.

2 **SEASON**
¹/₂ pound ground beef
2 teaspoons soy sauce, preferably dark

Stir the soy sauce into the meat.

3 **STIR-FRY**
2 tablespoons oil
4 cups cooked rice
pinch of salt

Heat oil in wok over high heat and add rice. Stir-fry vigorously for 3 to 5 minutes, breaking up clumps with the spatula turned down. Drizzle extra oil around the sides of the wok if the rice sticks excessively. Remove rice and set aside. Rinse wok.

4 **STIR-FRY**
2¹/₂ tablespoons oil

Heat wok over high heat. Add oil and let it get hot, then add onion. Stir-fry for 2 minutes, then add the seasoned beef. Stir-fry for 3 to 5 minutes.

5 **COMBINE-FRY**
1 egg, stirred

Add the rice. Toss together at a steady pace for 2 minutes. Pull the rice up the sides of the wok, leaving the center clear, then pour in the egg. Working within the cleared space, scramble the egg; when the egg is partially set, stir in the rice mixture and combine thoroughly. You will have little flecks of yellow scattered throughout the rice.

6 **SERVE**
soy sauce or hot sauce
cucumber sticks

Serve immediately with an extra dish of soy sauce or hot sauce to taste. Garnish with cucumber sticks.

NOTE: *A short-order wave of the magic wand and you'll take care of the nutritional concerns of your family by adding ¹/₂ to 1 cup of frozen green peas to the mixture as you stir-fry the meat (but leave out the onion). To make Pepperoni Fried Rice, instead of the ground beef, soy, and sherry, use 1 cup of pepperoni slices that have been cut in half. Add 1 tablespoon of tomato paste and a dash of salt at the end of your stir-fry.*

Dirty Wild Rice

 This recipe combines two American favorites—wild rice from the Minnesota bogs and rice flavored and colored with livers and gizzards, from southern Louisiana. You may also cut up some leftover roast meat and stir-fry that with the rice

SERVES 2 TO 4 PEOPLE

1 **COOK DUCK PARTS**
1 teaspoon black
   peppercorns
1 bay leaf
1 tablespoon
   Madeira
1 duck gizzard
1 duck liver

Fill a small saucepan with 1 inch of water and add the pepper, bay leaf, and wine. Add the gizzard and simmer for 30 minutes, then add the liver and simmer an additional 10 minutes. Remove from heat and allow to cool. Drain gizzards and reserve cooking liquid.

2 **COOK RICE**
¾ cup wild rice,
   rinsed
2 cups water

Drain thoroughly. Place rice in pot with water and gizzard cooking liquid. Bring to a boil, then cover and simmer for 25 minutes, or until rice is done.

3 **CUT**
3 cloves garlic
2 scallions

Peel and then slice the garlic very thin. Cut scallions into ⅛-inch rounds; keep the white and green parts separate. Cut the liver into thin slices. Shave the thick muscular membrane off the gizzard, then cut into the same size slices as the liver.

4 **STIR-FRY**
¼ cup oil; or 3
   tablespoons
   vegetable oil and
   1 tablespoon
   walnut oil

Heat oil in wok over medium heat. Fry the garlic slices until they turn light brown, then remove; they will crisp into chips. Add the scallion whites and stir-fry until they soften, about 1 minute.

5 **COMBINE-FRY**
1 egg, stirred

Add the rice to the wok and turn the mixture at a moderate pace. When the rice is aromatic, pour in the meat and toss to combine, about 2 minutes. Pull the rice up the sides of the wok, leaving the center bare. Pour in the egg and wait for the bottom to set. Then turn and scramble egg just a little. When egg is almost set, push down the rice and toss all together. Serve immediately with a sprinkle of the garlic chips and scallion greens on top.

Stir-fried Rice Vermicelli

Chinese rice vermicelli is pure white and thin as threads, with unmistakable crinkles in each strand. They can be turned into a quick meal, making a refreshing change from wheat noodles. I give here a popular combination of pork, cabbage, and bean sprouts. To this is added shreds of pickles or sweet gherkins for a tart twist (Asians would use a pickled mustard green, available in cans).

A steady stir-fry technique and patience are called for in this dish. The vermicelli tend to clump when stir-fried. You need to continuously toss them vigorously, sometimes frenetically. Also have at hand some extra oil and a bottle of water fitted with a spray nozzle or a bowl of water so you can splash the noodles as they cook. The noodles plump up and become enriched during the frying; and by slowly, constantly tossing the noodles and sprinkling them with water (like wetting laundry) you allow them to gradually absorb a rich toasted flavor. You could soak the noodles ahead to soften them, but the result is not quite the same—not as fragrant nor as firm, and certainly not so rich.

SERVES 2 TO 4 PEOPLE

---

1 **RINSE AND CUT**
2 cups bean sprouts
1/4 pound cabbage, green or savoy
1 pickle 4 inches long; or 1/2 cup pickled mustard greens
1/2 pound rice vermicelli
4 ounces boneless pork

Wash the bean sprouts in a sinkful of water and discard the hulls that float to the top. Shred cabbage into 2- and 4-inch segments. Seed pickle, then cut into thin strips the same size as cabbage. Cut vermicelli into 2- to 4-inch segments. Cut pork into shreds the same size.

---

2 **SEASON**
2 tablespoons light soy sauce
1 tablespoon sherry

Pour soy sauce and sherry over meat. Mix.

---

3 **STIR-FRY**
2 tablespoons oil
1 clove garlic

Heat wok over high heat and add oil. When oil is hot, render garlic and discard when slightly browned. Toss in meat and pickle and stir-fry until pork is cooked, about 45 seconds. Scoop out. Rinse wok.

---

4 **STIR-FRY**
2 tablespoons oil

Heat wok over high heat. Add oil to wok, allow to heat, and toss in cabbage. Stir-fry until pieces go limp, about 2 minutes, then add bean sprouts and turn mixture until sprouts are thoroughly heated, about 2 minutes.

5	**COMBINE-FRY**	Add meat mixture to wok and turn mixture to combine. Scoop out. Rinse wok.
6	**STIR-FRY** *½ cup plus 2 tablespoons oil, approximately* *½ cup water, approximately*	Immerse noodles in a large bowl of cold water and immediately take out, flinging off excess moisture. Heat 6 tablespoons oil in wok over medium heat. When oil is hot, add vermicelli and toss rapidly. Invert the spatula and use a fling-and-mop motion to prevent noodles from sticking and frying to a crisp. Splash in additional water in 4 to 5 installments and toss vigorously after each sprinkling. The water cools the wok and is also absorbed by the noodles. Drizzle additional oil around side of wok as needed; the wok should always be slick and shiny but not have excess oil. This operation takes about 20 minutes.
7	**COMBINE-FRY** *light soy sauce*	Pour in the stir-fried mixture and continue to turn for 2 minutes. Taste and adjust seasoning by adding soy sauce. Taste a noodle; it should not be brittle or hard but springy.
8	**SERVE** *hot sauce, preferably Siraja (see page 35)*	Remove from wok and serve immediately with a side dish of hot sauce. The crusty patches of noodle are especially prized.

New Year's Pasta

Although this recipe uses an East Asian pasta not commonly found in supermarkets, I include it here because it is a personal favorite as well as a favorite of all who love pasta dishes. Also sold as rice cake or rice sticks, the new year's cake is made from water-ground rice, a superfine and smooth flour. It is then formed into bars like gold bullion and steamed. After steaming it is sliced into long ⅛-inch-thick pieces before cooking. Fresh new year's cakes are available in season from some oriental groceries, but dried strips of the pasta are available year-round. Since the water-ground rice is fine and dense, five to seven days of soaking is necessary to thoroughly soften it. There is also a frozen type on the market but it does not fry well and it is only suitable for soup.

SERVES 2 TO 4 PEOPLE

---

1 | **SOAK**
2 cups dried new year's cake strips, or 1 pound fresh cake | If using dried strips, soak in a bowl of cold water for 5 to 7 days. Change water every day. If using fresh, slice on the diagonal into ⅛-inch pieces and soak in cold water for 30 minutes.

---

2 | **CUT AND SEASON**
8 ounces boneless pork
½ to ¾ pound napa cabbage
1½ tablespoons light soy sauce
1 tablespoon sherry | Slice pork across the grain into pieces the size of the pasta. Cut cabbage into pieces ½ inch wide and 2 inches long, or about the size of the pasta. Keep the stem and leaf pieces separate. Pour the soy sauce and sherry over the meat. Mix.

---

3 | **STIR-FRY**
2 tablespoons oil
⅛ teaspoon salt | Heat wok over high heat and add oil. When oil is hot, toss in the stem sections of the cabbage and stir-fry. When they are hot, pour in the leafy sections and toss at a steady pace for 1 minute. Add the salt and continue to turn the mixture until the thickest stem sections are thoroughly cooked, about 3 minutes. Scoop out onto a plate. Wipe wok.

---

4 | **STIR-FRY**
2 tablespoons oil
1 clove garlic | Heat wok over high heat. Add oil, allow to get hot, and render garlic in hot oil. Remove when slightly brown and discard. Add the meat and stir-fry for a few seconds.

---

5 | **COMBINE-FRY** | When the meat has turned white, add the cabbage and turn mixture to combine. Scoop out and clean wok.

6 **STIR-FRY**
6 tablespoons oil,
approximately

Drain the pasta. Heat oil in wok over high heat. When oil is hot add the pasta, swirling additional oil (about 2 tablespoons) down the sides as you stir-fry to keep the pasta from sticking. The pieces will begin to glue to each other; poke the corner of the spatula into a piece of the pasta. If it is tender throughout, the pasta is cooked.

7 **COMBINE-FRY**
hot sauce

Immediately pour in the pork and cabbage mixture. The juices from the vegetable and meat will help to re-separate the pasta pieces. Turn to combine and allow the pasta to absorb the juices and gravy, about 45 seconds. Serve immediately. Offer hot sauce.

Shrimp and Bean Sprout Lo-mein

 A winning combination.

SERVES 4 PEOPLE

1	**COOK** 1 pound fresh wheat noodles; or ¾ pound dried	Bring a large pot of water to a boil. Add noodles and cook at a full boil until noodles are firm but tender. Drain and rinse with cold water until cool.
2	**PEEL AND SEASON** 1½ cups medium shrimp 1 tablespoon light soy sauce 1 tablespoon sherry 2 teaspoons cornstarch	Peel and devein the shrimp. Split in half lengthwise. Mix seasonings into shrimp.
3	**RINSE AND CUT** ½ pound bean sprouts 1 cup fresh or frozen green beans	Put sprouts in a sinkful of cold water. Skim off husks and roots that float to the top. Drain. Cut fresh beans on the diagonal.
4	**STIR-FRY** 3 tablespoons oil 1 slice gingerroot 1 tablespoon cornstarch ¼ cup soy sauce ¼ cup water	Heat oil in wok over high heat. Render garlic in hot oil, then discard when it begins to brown. Pour in the shrimp and toss. When shrimp have just turned pink, add the sprouts and beans. Turn the mixture until sprouts are wilted but still crisp, about 2 minutes. Combine cornstarch with soy sauce and water, then pour over mixture in wok. Turn mixture continuously until liquid thickens and becomes clear. Scoop out. Rinse wok.
5	**STIR-FRY** ½ cup oil	Heat oil in wok over high heat. Add noodles and turn in the oil, stir-frying until well coated with oil and thoroughly heated.
6	**SEASON AND SERVE** 3 tablespoons soy sauce hot sauce	Pour in the shrimp mixture and turn to combine. Add soy sauce to taste and serve immediately, with hot sauce on side.

New Year's Pasta

PAGES 120-121

Free-form Lasagna

PAGES 128-129

Rotini with Ragù Rosa

This is a honest, hearty sauce. The meat is not ground, but diced; it is a sauce you can put your teeth into, and you can put it over any kind of noodle you wish.

SERVES 4 PEOPLE

1 CUT
1 medium onion
½ medium carrot
1 stalk celery
2 cloves garlic
4 cups canned
    tomatoes, with
    juice
¾ pound boneless
    pork loin
¾ pound boneless
    beef chuck

Cut onion in half across the grain, then into slivers. Dice the carrot and celery. Mince the garlic. Drain the tomatoes, saving the juice; squeeze out seeds and chop. Cut meat into ½-inch dice, being sure to include some pork fat as well.

2 STIR-FRY
¼ cup olive oil
2 tablespoons butter

Heat the olive oil and butter in wok over medium heat. Add onion, carrot, celery, and garlic and stir-fry until onion is limp. Add the meat and toss at a moderate pace until it turns color, about 2 minutes.

3 SIMMER
1 cup red wine
1 cup beef stock
6 sprigs parsley
pinch of mace
pinch of ground
    cinnamon
½ teaspoon each
    dried oregano
    and basil
salt and pepper to
    taste

Add wine, stock, and tomatoes, along with tomato liquid, then add seasonings to wok and cover. Bring to a boil and let mixture barely simmer. Cook for 1½ hours, but check periodically. If liquid is cooking down too fast, add more wine or stock. After sauce has cooked, remove lid and turn up heat to evaporate any excess liquid and to thicken sauce.

4 BOIL
1 pound rotini pasta

Bring a large pot of water to a boil and add the pasta. Cook until done but firm, *al dente,* about 10 minutes. Drain and serve with sauce poured over.

Beef Lo-mein

Lo-mein is the ultimate meal-in-one. It is pasta, meat, and vegetable in a tidy dish. And it fixes in a flash. With a knowledge of stir-fry in your hands, you can cook up variation upon variation of this fundamental favorite. Following is a recipe for lo-mein made with beef and broccoli. It is the foremost combination consumed in my household.

SERVES 4 PEOPLE

---

1 | **COOK**
1 pound fresh wheat noodles; or ¾ pound dried | Bring a large pot of water to boil and add noodles. Cook in vigorously boiling water until firm but tender, then drain and rinse thoroughly with cold water until cooled.

---

2 | **CUT AND SEASON**
1 bunch broccoli
¾ pound flank steak
2 tablespoons soy sauce | Peel broccoli stalks. Cut on the diagonal into ⅛- to ¼-inch slices. Split flowerets lengthwise so that no stem is thicker than ¼ inch. Cut meat across the grain into ⅛- to ¼-inch-thick slices; they should be the same size as the broccoli stems. Add soy sauce to meat and mix.

---

3 | **STIR-FRY**
3 tablespoons oil
½ cup water or chicken stock | Heat 3 tablespoons oil in wok over high heat. Stir-fry broccoli until bright green, then splash water in and cover to steam the vegetable lightly, about 1 minute. Scoop out broccoli and liquid. Wipe wok clean.

---

4 | **STIR-FRY**
2 tablespoons oil
1 clove garlic | Heat oil in wok over high heat. Render garlic, then remove when just browned. Toss in meat and mop and fling it against the sides of the wok.

---

5 | **COMBINE-FRY**
2 tablespoons cornstarch
2 tablespoons water | When beef has lost most of its red color, add the broccoli. Stir together the cornstarch and water, making sure there is no sediment. Pour into the wok, turning continuously. The gravy will thicken and turn translucent. Scoop out and set aside. Rinse wok.

---

6 | **STIR-FRY**
6 tablespoons oil | Heat oil in wok over high heat. Pour in the noodles and stir-fry over medium heat, turning them in the oil so they are well-coated with the oil and heated. Pour the meat and broccoli mixture into the wok and turn the entire mixture to combine evenly.

7 ***SEASON AND SERVE***
2 tablespoons oyster
sauce or soy sauce
hot bean paste,
Tabasco, or Siraja
sauce (see
Ingredients)

Splash the oyster sauce or soy sauce over the mixture in wok. Turn and toss in. If the noodles are not salty enough, add more. Serve with one of the hot sauces.

Tomato Sauce Lo-mein

 Don't let names bother you. Call this vermicelli or linguine, or fettuccine with meat sauce, if you prefer. But do experiment with Asian wheat noodles, because they offer a huge variety and will give your favorite dishes a refreshingly new twist. We have Marco Polo's accounts to assure us that this cross-cultural noodling has historical validity.

SERVES 4 PEOPLE

---

1 | **COOK**
¾ *pound dried wheat noodles, or 1 pound fresh* | Bring water to a boil in a large pot or the wok, and cook noodles just until firm but done. Drain immediately and cool with cold running water.

---

2 | **CUT**
½ *to 1 pound piece flank or round steak*
1 onion
1 clove garlic
1 pound ripe tomatoes; or 1 can (23 ounces) whole tomatoes | Cut meat across the grain into strips ⅛ inch thick and 2½ inches long. Then cut again so meat slivers are same width as noodles. Set aside. Slice the onion. Mince the garlic. Peel, seed, and chop the fresh tomatoes.

---

3 | **STIR-FRY**
2 tablespoons oil | Heat oil in wok over high heat. When oil is hot, add meat and stir-fry until no longer pink, about 3 to 5 minutes. Scoop out and set aside. Rinse wok.

---

4 | **STIR-FRY**
1½ tablespoons olive oil
2 tablespoons butter
3 tablespoons tomato paste | Heat oil in wok over high heat and add butter. When hot, toss in onion and garlic and stir-fry until onion softens. Add tomatoes and tomato paste. Turn steadily until mixture bubbles.

5   SIMMER

3 tablespoons
    Madeira
1 bouillon cube
2 teaspoons fish
    sauce (optional)
1/2 cup red wine
1/2 teaspoon dried
    oregano
2 teaspoons dried
    mint
salt and pepper to
    taste
1/2 teaspoon cayenne

Add the Madeira and bouillon cube to the wok. Add fish sauce if desired (it will not give a fishy taste, but will add depth). Add wine, herbs, and season with salt, pepper, and cayenne. Cover and let mixture simmer for 10 minutes. Uncover and turn a few times while sauce cooks; it should be a little on the watery side.

6   COMBINE-FRY

grated parmesan
    cheese

Add meat to the sauce and bring to a boil. As soon as it returns to boil, add the noodles. Turn the mixture until well combined, then serve immediately, with a sprinkling of grated parmesan cheese.

Free-form Lasagna

 This recipe does not hope to be an authentic lasagna; rather, it is a different version of the traditional favorite, made quickly and easily in a wok. The sauce does not need to be simmered for hours; everything is made and assembled in one cooking utensil; and eggroll or wonton squares contribute a softer texture. If you use fresh ingredients and good seasonings, you will have all the elements that make lasagna taste good.

Like many rapid-fire dishes, this one demands a bit of technical confidence, but I prefer to think of it more as a daredevil attitude than cooking knowledge because the methods are not difficult. Moreover, remember the title "free-form" as you make it, and tell your family or friends, "This was made in a wok."

SERVES 4 TO 6 PEOPLE

1

CUT
1 onion
1 clove garlic
1 can (23 ounces)
  whole tomatoes

Slice the onion. Mince the garlic. Drain the tomatoes, then pick each tomato up and quickly squeeze the seeds out; you don't have to be too thorough in removing all the seeds, but don't cut tomatoes.

2

STIR-FRY
1½ tablespoons olive
  oil
2 tablespoons butter
3 tablespoons tomato
  paste
½ cup red wine

Heat oil in wok and add butter. When hot, toss in onion and garlic and stir-fry over high heat until onion softens. When onion is soft, add tomatoes. Invert, then chop tomatoes with the tip of the spatula to cut them up into small pieces. Pour in the wine and let the mixture bubble for about 3 minutes.

3

SIMMER
1 beef bouillon cube
2 teaspoons fish
  sauce (optional)
3 tablespoons
  Madeira
½ teaspoon dried
  oregano
2 teaspoons chopped
  fresh mint
salt and pepper to
  taste
½ teaspoon cayenne

Add bouillon cube and fish sauce, if desired. (It will not give a fishy taste, but will add depth.) Add Madeira, herbs, and seasonings to taste. Cover and let mixture simmer for 15 minutes. Uncover and turn mixture a few times while sauce cooks; it should be a little on the thin side.

4	**COOK** *4 quarts water* *1 tablespoon oil* *1 pound eggroll* *wrappers*	While the sauce simmers, bring water to a boil in a large pot and add the oil. Cut the stack of eggroll wrappers in half so you have strips 3 inches wide and 6 inches long. Shuffle the stack of noodles like a ream of paper; this helps separate them. Put noodles in boiling water and stir, doing your best to keep them separate, but don't worry if some stick together. As soon as the water returns to a boil, pour the entire pot into a colander. Drain and cool with running water. When the noodles are cool enough to handle, separate them under running water. (So long as most are single or double thickness, they are fine; if some are thoroughly cooked, do not be alarmed.)
5	**ADD** *2 tablespoons olive* *oil*	When sauce is ready, add noodles and immediately drizzle the oil over them. Then gently turn the noodles in the sauce a few times. Cover, adding a little water to the mixture if it seems dry. Cook for 2 to 4 minutes, letting the sauce bubble gently.
6	**ASSEMBLE** *½ pound ricotta* *¼ pound* *mozzarella cheese,* *grated* *¼ pound parmesan* *cheese, grated* *½ cup water*	Working quickly, remove two-thirds of the noodles from the wok and place on a shallow work dish or the platter on which you will eventually serve the lasagna. The one-third noodle-sauce mixture still in the wok is the bottom layer of your lasagna. Sprinkle that mixture with half the cheeses. Lay on top another third of sauce with noodles, then the remainder of the cheeses, and top with the final third of the noodles. Turn heat up and drizzle a circle of water around the lasagna. Lift the edges up (like peeking under a pancake to see if it is done) so the water can slide down. Cover wok and turn heat to medium-high. In about 3 minutes, lift and peek at bottom again; it should begin to brown. Drizzle more water in if it threatens to burn, but remember that you are encouraging the bottom to brown. The mixture should be slightly bubbling, and you should see the cheese melting at the edges. If not, turn up the heat; cover; and let cook again—this process heats the total mixture and lets the bottom brown.
7	**SERVE**	Remove portions of lasagna from the wok by using your spatula. Flip them over onto the plates so the crusty noodles are on top. Serve with additional grated parmesan cheese.
		NOTE: *If desired, move the lasagna in one piece to your normal lasagne baking dish. Shape and thump the mass to fill the dish, then sprinkle with parmesan cheese and run dish under the broiler to melt cheese and brown the top further.*

Quick Cannelloni

Ready-made eggroll or wonton wrappers are used here to wrap a filling that does not need to be pre-cooked, so the usually time-consuming Italian favorite is prepared in half the time. I prefer wonton wrappers because they make daintier, neater rolls.

SERVES 4 TO 6 PEOPLE

---

1   **BECHAMEL SAUCE**
4 tablespoons
   unsalted butter
3 tablespoons flour
2 cups milk
1 teaspoon salt

In a small saucepan, melt butter and then add flour. Stir until the butter bubbles. Add milk, stirring all the while, and continue to cook over medium heat until the sauce thickens and begins to bubble again. Add salt to taste. Set aside.

---

2   **TOMATO SAUCE**
1 recipe Ragù Rosa
   sauce (page 125)
   or Tomato Sauce
   (page 126)

Prepare sauce and set aside.

---

3   **MIX**
½ pound ground
   beef
1 package (10
   ounces) frozen
   chopped spinach,
   thawed
3 shallots, finely
   chopped
¼ cup olive oil,
   heated to almost
   smoking
1 cup ricotta
salt and pepper to
   taste
1 cup grated
   parmesan cheese

Mix meat and spinach in a heatproof mixing bowl. Place shallots centered over meat, then pour oil directly on them. The shallots will sizzle. Stir into meat. Add ricotta, ½ cup bechamel sauce, salt and pepper, and parmesan cheese and mix together.

4	**ASSEMBLE** *10 eggroll wrappers,* *or 20 wonton* *wrappers*	Butter a baking dish which will fit onto the steaming rack or a steaming plate. (You may need 2 dishes and stagger the steaming.) Place a wrapper on the work surface in front of you. Spoon filling (about 3 tablespoons for eggroll wrapper, 1 tablespoon for wonton wrapper) in the middle. Roll the filling into a log shape. With the seam facing down, place on buttered dish and continue for remaining wrappers and filling.
5	**STEAM**	Bring water to a boil in wok, with rack in place. Steam cannelloni over high heat for 20 minutes. While steaming, reheat both sauces.
6	**BROIL** *½ cup grated* *parmesan cheese* *4 tablespoons butter*	Remove steaming dish and rack from wok. Pour off excess water, if some collected in baking dish. Pour the remainder of the bechamel sauce over rolls in dish and cover with all the tomato sauce. Sprinkle with cheese and dot with butter. Broil on medium rack in broiler until sauces bubble and cheese has browned a little on top.

Paprika Pork with Thumbprint Noodles

 "Thumbprint" refers to the way in which the noodles are made. The dough is held over the simmering stew; you tear off pieces between your thumb and index finger and drop them directly into the cooking liquid. Although you could use any of several kinds of dough (leftover pie crust, biscuit dough and so on), the following is a very lean dough, made simply from flour, water, and salt. Soaking the paprika in water allows its flavor to blossom more fully.

SERVES 4 TO 6 PEOPLE

1	**MIX AND KNEAD** 2 cups all-purpose flour ¾ cup boiling water	Place flour in a bowl and pour boiling water in, stirring as you add it. Continue to stir until dough balls up. Allow to cool slightly, then knead until smooth. Cover with a damp cloth until stew is ready.
2	**SOAK** 1 tablespoon paprika, preferably imported Hungarian 2 tablespoons water	Place paprika in water and leave to soak while you prepare the meat. It will become pastelike, then swell to a stiffer consistency.
3	**CUT** 2 pounds boneless pork, preferably Boston butt 2 small onions	Cut meat into ¼-inch strips. Cut each onion into 8 pieces.
4	**STIR-FRY** 2 tablespoons oil	Heat wok over high heat and add oil. When oil is hot, add onions and stir-fry until soft, about 3 minutes. Remove. Rinse wok.
5	**STIR-FRY** 3 tablespoons oil, approximately 1 clove garlic 2 tablespoons tomato paste	Pour in 3 remaining tablespoons oil and render garlic until it turns brown. Discard. Add meat to wok and toss quickly, then scoop out, leaving oil. Add the paprika paste and turn mixture in wok over medium heat. Add tomato paste and turn to mix with paprika. (Add more oil if necessary to keep mixture from sticking.)
6	**COMBINE-FRY**	Add the meat to the wok. Coat with paste and add onions.

7 STEW
2 cups chicken or
  beef stock,
  approximately
salt and pepper
1/8 teaspoon ground
  cinnamon
pinch each of
  nutmeg, allspice,
  cloves
1 star anise

Pour in the stock and add seasonings to taste. Bring mixture to a boil, cover, and cook over medium heat for 45 minutes or until tender. Check the stew to make sure it is just simmering. Add stock to replenish what evaporates during cooking.

8 ADD
freshly ground black
  pepper

Just before serving, bring cooking liquid back to a boil. Tear off bite-size pieces of dough with your fingers and drop into the gravy. Work fast; when all dough is in, stir and cover. Cook for 2 minutes, adding more stock if the mixture is too thick. Check and taste noodles to see if done; they should be chewy. The starch given off by the noodles will also thicken the liquid, providing gravy. Remove star anise and serve hot with several twists of the pepper-mill.

Braised Shrimp

The "braised" in the title of this recipe is deceptive. Like many wok-simmered dishes, it means a matter of 5 or 10 minutes of cooking with the lid on. If you are fortunate and can purchase whole shrimp, prepare them by cutting off the antennae and horns with kitchen shears—that is, cut off the first ¼ inch of the tip of the head.

SERVES 2 TO 4 PEOPLE

---

1 | **CLEAN** | Devein the shrimp by cutting with shears through the shell
| 1 pound headed | along the upper ridge of the flesh. Take out the exposed
| shrimp, or 1¼ | vein.
| pounds with heads |

---

2 | **CUT** | Cut scallions into rounds up through the stalk sections;
| 1 bunch scallions | leave off the dark green tops. Mince the garlic and gin-
| 1 clove garlic | ger.
| 2 slices gingerroot |

---

3 | **STIR-FRY** | Heat oil in wok. When oil is hot, add scallions, garlic, and
| 3 tablespoons oil | ginger. When the scallions are softened, add the shrimp.
| | Toss at a moderate pace until they turn red, about
| | 2 minutes.

---

4 | **BRAISE** | Add the soy sauces. Turn mixture and let healthy brown
| 3 tablespoons dark | color permeate. Then add the sherry, vinegar, sugar, and
| soy sauce | water. Cover and let mixture come to a boil, then reduce
| 2 teaspoons light soy | heat to simmer for about 5 minutes. Then lift off lid and stir
| sauce | mixture. Turn heat to high and bring back to a rapid boil.
| 1 tablespoon sherry | Let liquid boil and toss shrimp at a moderate pace until
| 1 teaspoon zijiang | liquid begins to reduce and concentrate in color, about
| or cider vinegar | 5 minutes. Serve immediately with plain rice, or refrigerate
| 1 teaspoon sugar | overnight and reheat by tossing in wok; or serve cold, espe-
| ⅓ cup water | cially as an appetizer.

Smothered Fish

I return to this recipe whenever I encounter little whole fish or scallions on sale during my marketing foray. Sea bass, porgies, or whiting about 8 to 9 inches in length are best for this dish; fillets will not work. When refrigerated overnight and served cold, this dish is also excellent as a small course, served with toast points.

SERVES 2 TO 4 PEOPLE

1 CLEAN AND TRIM
6 to 8 small whole fish, dressed
4 to 6 bunches scallions

Check that fish are well scaled. Leave the tails and heads on if possible. Rinse and dry thoroughly with paper towels. Cut off roots from scallions. Strip off outer leaves if not firm. Holding each scallion as if it were a 12-inch length of twine, tie a knot in its center. (This prevents scallion from disintegrating and fraying as it stews.)

2 FRY
¼ cup oil, approximately
2 slices gingerroot

Have wok absolutely dry and hot before adding oil (there is much less chance of fish sticking this way). When oil is hot, render ginger and discard when browned at edges. Slip fish in and fry on each side for 2 to 3 minutes, nudging occasionally. Add more oil if necessary to prevent sticking. Remove fish and set aside.

3 STIR-FRY
1 to 2 tablespoons oil

Add scallions to wok and pour in a little more oil to coat them. Stir-fry scallions until they wilt, about 3 minutes, then return fish to wok.

4 BRAISE
2 tablespoons light soy sauce
¼ cup dark soy sauce
2 tablespoons sherry
2 teaspoons zijiang or cider vinegar
1 teaspoon sugar
½ cup water, approximately

Pour in sauces and turn fish and scallions to coat them. Let the brown liquid penetrate a little, then add the sherry, vinegar, sugar, and water to the wok. Turn ingredients at a leisurely pace, then move the scallions so that half of them are massed over the fish. Add more water if necessary to barely cover fish, then cover wok and bring to a boil. Turn heat to medium, and simmer for 15 minutes. Check after 10 minutes and turn ingredients. Adjust the heat so that the mixture is just simmering. After 20 minutes, turn the heat to high and remove lid. The cooking liquid will reduce and the gravy turn a deeper brown. Nudge and lift the contents with the spatula to prevent burning at hot spots.

5 SERVE

Remove contents to a serving dish and mass the scallions on top. Accompany with bread or rice. Or refrigerate dish overnight to fuse flavors. Reheat the next day to serve hot. If serving cold, break up congealed liquid slightly and mound some jelled gravy and onions over fish for a rustic aspic.

Fish Fillets Piperade

 Piperade *is a French regional specialty made chiefly of peppers and tomatoes. The natural aroma of cooked peppers and the fruity tartness and sweetness of tomatoes make it a perfect foil to lightly fried fish fillets.**

SERVES 4

1 | **CUT and GRATE**
4 bell peppers
5 medium tomatoes; or 1 can (23 ounces) whole peeled tomatoes
2 cloves garlic
2 shallots
4 ounces gruyère cheese

Seed the peppers, then sliver into ¼-inch strips. Peel and seed the tomatoes and section into eighths. Peel and mince the shallots and garlic. Grate the cheese. Set aside.

2 | **SEASON**
4 trout or sole fillets, about 2 pounds total
2 tablespoons dry vermouth
½ teaspoon salt
pinch each of black pepper and cayenne
1 clove garlic, pressed
1 shallot, pressed
½ teaspoon each minced fresh oregano and basil; or ¼ each teaspoon dried

Set fish fillets in a dish. Combine remaining ingredients and over the fish. Make sure both sides of each fillet are seasoned by rubbing in the seasonings with your fingertips. Let stand while you prepare to deep-fry.

4 | **PREHEAT**
3 cups oil
½ cup cornstarch

Heat oil in wok, until 370 degrees. Place the cornstarch on a sheet of wax paper close to the stove.

5	**COMBINE** *½ cup white flour* *1 egg* *½ cup very cold* *water*	This batter must be as cold as possible when it goes into the hot oil. Place the flour in a 3- to 4-cup bowl or cup. Break the egg into it. Stir with a fork while you pour the water into the flour. Stop as soon as the mixture is blended and do not attempt to take out the lumps.
6	**DEEP-FRY**	When the oil is ready, pick up a piece of fish by the tip, lower it onto the cornstarch, then flip it over so that both sides are coated. Lift and shake off excess starch. Immediately dip into the cold batter and then ease the fillet into the oil. (The powdering, dipping, and frying procedure should take place in one sweep.) Fry 2 fillets at a time. As soon as they turn golden, remove with the perforated ladle and drain on paper towels. Keep warm.
7	**STIR-FRY** *3 tablespoons olive* *oil* *3 tablespoons butter* *1 clove garlic,* *minced* *1 shallot, chopped* *salt and pepper* *2 teaspoons minced* *fresh parsley; or 1* *teaspoon dried* *⅛ teaspoon oregano*	When all fillets are fried, pour off the oil, leaving about 1 tablespoon in wok. Add the olive oil and butter and return to the stove. Stir-fry the reserved garlic and shallots, and when they soften, add the peppers and toss until they wilt, about 5 minutes. Then pour in the tomatoes and add parsley and oregano. Turn the mixture until the sauce reaches a thick consistency almost of jam with no excess moisture. Pour in the grated cheese and give the mixture 2 turns in the wok.
8	**SERVE**	Scoop the piperade over the fish fillets and serve immediately.

*Improvisation not recommended; use all measurements as given.

Flounder with Meat Sauce

While the fish steams, slivers of meat, mushrooms, and scallions are quickly stir-fried. When the fish is done, the savory sauce is poured over.

SERVES 2 PEOPLE

1 **SOAK**
2 black mushrooms

Place mushrooms in a small bowl of cold water to soften while you proceed with recipe.

2 **PREPARE**
1½ pound dressed flounder or other white fish
4 tablespoons sherry
3 scallions, cut in 2-inch segments
3 slices gingerroot

Check for stray scales. Rinse, especially the cavity, and pat dry. Score the fish on both sides with 2 to 3 diagonal cuts. Bruise scallion pieces and ginger with the blade of a knife, then combine with sherry in a bowl. Bathe fish in this mixture, rubbing the cavity well with the soaked ginger and scallion pieces. Place fish in steaming dish.

3 **CUT AND SEASON**
4 ounces boneless pork
2 scallions
1 clove garlic
2 tablespoons light soy sauce
1 tablespoon sherry

Cut meat into slivers and scallions into 2-inch segments then split the scallion segments lengthwise into quarters. Sliver garlic. Cut stems off softened mushrooms and discard. Sliver to the same size as the meat and scallions. Pour soy sauce and sherry into the meat and mix.

4 **STEAM**

Bring water to a boil in the wok, with rack in place. Steam fish over high heat for 8 to 10 minutes, or until done.

5 **STIR-FRY**
1½ tablespoons oil

While fish steams, heat oil in a second wok or frying pan over high heat. Toss in the scallions and stir-fry. When the aroma is apparent, add the mushrooms and pork. Toss; your stir-fry should be done at about the same time as the fish. Test fish and, if done, lift dish onto a larger platter. Pour pork mixture over and serve immediately.

Meatcake with Salt Cod
Served with Steamed Buns

PAGES 140-141

Chicken and Snow Peas

PAGE 142

Stuffed Squid

Pork and squid would seem to make strange bedfellows, but this combination is steamed for a rich dish of complementary textures and flavors.

SERVES 2 TO 4 PEOPLE

---

1   **CLEAN AND SEASON**
4 to 8 medium
    squid, no longer
    than 8 inches in
    body
1 slice gingerroot
2 scallions
2 tablespoons sherry

Clean squid by removing the innards entirely. Peel off the thin speckled membrane. Lightly bruise the scallions and ginger slice, and toss with the squid and wine. Slash lengthwise so squid become boat-shaped containers.

---

2   **STUFF**
¾ pound ground
    pork
1 clove garlic,
    minced
2 tablespoons
    minced Sichuan
    kohlrabi
1 tablespoon soy
    sauce
1 tablespoon sherry
½ teaspoon salt

Combine stuffing ingredients in a bowl and mix. Stuff into the squid and place in a soup plate.

---

3   **STEAM**

Bring water to a boil in the wok, with rack in place. Steam squid over medium high heat for 30 minutes. Check wok intermittently; if water level is low, add boiling water. After 30 minutes, taste squid. If it is not yet tender, steam a little longer. Serve with plain rice and sauce with steaming gravy.

Meatcake with Salt Cod
Served with Steamed Buns

 This dish is simplicity itself. The steam cooks both the meatcake studded with slivers of salt cod and the sweet, plain steamed buns that accompany the dish. In short order, you have a dish of rustic flavors that can be enjoyed just as directly—by dunking the buns in the gravy or wrapping them around the meatcake. The contrast of the salty meat and fish cake makes the bun taste sweeter than bread has ever tasted.

SERVES 4 PEOPLE

1 **MIX**
1 tablespoon sugar
2 teaspoons active
   dry yeast
1¾ cups warm
   water
2 tablespoons oil
5 to 6 cups
   all-purpose flour

Combine the sugar and yeast in a large bowl with the warm water. Let yeast proof—foam up—for about 10 minutes, then stir the oil into the yeast mixture. Add the flour, kneading it in until all is absorbed. Place dough on a flat surface and knead until elastic, about 8 minutes. (This kneading can also be done in a food processor.)

2 **LET RISE**

Place dough in a greased bowl, cover with a damp cloth, and let rise in a warm place until doubled or tripled in volume, about 1½ hours.

3 **SHAPE**

Punch dough down, remove from bowl, and knead into a firm ball. Let rest for 5 minutes, then form into a long log the size of a loaf of French bread. Cut into 1-inch chunks. Cut parchment paper or foil into 3-inch squares. Flatten each hunk of dough by mashing the dough with the palm of your hand. Fold the dough in half over itself and place on the squares.

4 **LET RISE**

Place rolls on plates, bamboo disks, or racks. Make sure there is plenty of room around for the rolls to rise—not more than 5 or 6 rolls to an 8-inch plate. Cover with a damp cloth and let rise until doubled, about 1 hour.

5 **SOAK**
1 piece (2 inches)
   salt cod fillet

Rinse salt off the fish, then place in a bowl of cold water. Let soak for about 1 hour.

6 **CUT AND SEASON**
$\frac{3}{4}$ *pound boneless*
pork, preferably
Boston butt; or $\frac{3}{4}$
pound ground
pork
1 clove garlic
1 tablespoon sherry
1 tablespoon light
soy sauce

Cut pork into thin slices, then mince by hand or in a food processor; be sure to include some fat. Drain fish and cut cod into thin slices, then chop into fine, tiny pieces. Combine the pork and fish in a steaming dish. Squeeze garlic through a press over pork, and pour in the sherry and soy sauce; then mix in well. Combine and press into a flat, uniformly thick cake in the steaming dish.

7 **STEAM**

Heat water in a wok, with steaming rack in place. Steam both buns and cake at the same time if you have stacking bamboo steaming racks, or do each individually. Steam buns for 10 minutes, cake for 15 to 20 minutes. (If steaming individually, reheat buns for 1 minute in steamer before serving.)

8 **SERVE**

Serve cake with steaming juices that collect in dish, accompanied by buns. Break off a sizeable chunk of the meat patty and fold a piece of bun around it, or hold the bread in one hand while you eat the cake with a fork or chopsticks. Dunk the bun in the juices, too.

Chicken and Snow Peas

 Although snow peas have a crisp texture and complement any meat in a stir-fry, I find them one of the few vegetables delicate enough for chicken. The egg white and cornstarch in this recipe create a thin film that seals off the chicken from direct contact with the oil, producing a chicken meat with a silky finesse. The fancy way is to cook the chicken pieces first in a lot of medium-hot oil, which cooks but does not deep-fry the coating; here is the everyday method—simply to stir-fry the chicken separately from the peas, then combine and fry them together.

SERVES 2 TO 4 PEOPLE

1	**TRIM** ½ *pound young snow peas*	String the peas from the stem ends. Cut peas on the diagonal in half.
2	**CUT AND SEASON** 1 *whole chicken breast* ½ *egg white* ¼ *teaspoon salt* ½ *tablespoon cornstarch*	Take meat off the bone and remove skin. Remove tendons by scraping the meat off with a sharp knife. Slice breast pieces with the grain into slices ⅛ inch thick. Mix the egg white, salt, and cornstarch into the chicken pieces in a bowl and refrigerate for 1 hour.
3	**STIR-FRY** 1 *tablespoon oil* *salt*	Heat oil in wok set over high heat. Toss in the snow peas and stir-fry at a steady pace for 2 to 3 minutes, season with salt, and then scoop out and set aside. Wipe wok.
4	**STIR-FRY** ¼ *cup oil*	Heat oil in wok over high heat. When very hot, toss the chicken in and stir-fry vigorously, using the fling-and-mop motion to separate the pieces.
5	**COMBINE-FRY** *white pepper*	Add the snow peas and toss quickly. Immediately pour onto serving plates and dust with some white pepper. Serve with rice.

Brown Chicken

A whole chicken, split down its back, nestles perfectly in the bowl of a wok. In this very simple treatment, the chicken cooks in a rich soy sauce stock. When finished, the skin is imbued with a chocolate brown while the flesh stays a moist, clean white. Total cooking time is 50 minutes or less, and it requires very little tending. Best of all, it can be cooked ahead served at room temperature.

SERVES 4 PEOPLE

---

1 BOIL

1/4 cup dark soy sauce
1 1/2 tablespoons light soy sauce
1 tablespoon sugar
1 star anise
1/2 teaspoon 5-spice powder
1 tablespoon sherry
1 1/2 cups water

Place ingredients in wok and bring to a boil over high heat. Stir initially to dissolve the sugar, then let mixture reach an active boil.

---

2 CUT

1 frying chicken, 2 1/2 to 3 pounds

Split bird down one side of backbone. Open up and cut backbone off other side. Use a little force to press the 2 halves wide open; the chicken must nestle in the curve of the wok.

---

3 COOK

Slip chicken skin side up into boiling stock and add water if necessary so that thigh and leg portions are immersed. Cover wok and bring liquid to a boil again. Turn heat to medium and continue to cook with lid on for 40 minutes. Nudge chicken to avoid scorching when it may come in contact with a hot spot on the wok. Press thigh joint with a fork or knife; if the juices flow out clear, chicken is done. Turn skin side up and cook another 5 minutes without lid on. The cooking liquid will reduce a little.

---

4 SERVE

Remove chicken. If serving warm, let rest for 10 minutes before cutting. If serving at room temperature, let chicken cool completely, then cut. Strain stock and serve with chicken and plain rice.

Butter-glazed Chicken and Onions

 A robust stew that takes 45 minutes to prepare. Butter and onions pick up a richness and sweetness with the hearty dark soy sauce and the little bit of sugar helps the gravy shine with a healthy brown color.

SERVES 4 PEOPLE

1 | **CUT**
8 medium onions
1 frying chicken,
about 3 pounds

Peel and quarter onions. Cut chicken into 4 breast and leg sections, or chop through bone into 1½-inch-wide pieces. The flavors penetrate the chicken meat more fully and the juices and bone marrow flow to the gravy to enrich it if the chicken is chopped.

2 | **STIR-FRY**
3 tablespoons oil

Heat 3 tablespoons oil in wok over high heat. When oil is hot, add onions and stir-fry at a leisurely pace until they soften. Take out. Wipe wok.

3 | **STIR-FRY**
2 tablespoons oil

Heat oil in wok over high heat. Add the chicken pieces. Stir-fry the thighs and legs for 1 minute, then the breast and remaining pieces at a leisurely pace until the skin is cooked.

4 | **BRAISE**
3 tablespoons dark
soy sauce
2 tablespoons light
soy sauce
2 tablespoons sugar
¼ cup water

Add soy sauces and sugar to wok and turn to coat chicken. Keep turning to let color penetrate the skin—about 2 minutes. Pour in the water and add the onions. Turn the mixture a few times, then cover and bring liquid to an active boil. Turn heat to medium and simmer for 25 minutes. Check in 10 to 15 minutes and turn the mixture a few times. Moving the pieces of chicken prevents scorching and sticking at the hot spots. Check again at 5- to 10-minute intervals.

5 | **REDUCE AND GLAZE**
6 tablespoons butter

Preheat the broiler. Add 4 tablespoons butter to the braising mixture and adjust the heat to high. Turn the mixture as it boils; the liquid will reduce quickly. Begin to turn more vigorously as the gravy cooks down to the lower fourth of the stew; this should take 7 to 10 minutes. When liquid is reduced, scoop out chicken and onions and place onto a shallow baking dish. There should be about ½ to ¾ cup braising liquid left. With the spatula, spoon it and the onions over the chicken, dot chicken with remaining butter, and place dish under broiler until butter is melted and sauce is bubbling. Serve with plain rice.

Thai Chicken in Green Curry

Green curry paste is pounded fresh green chilies, and these make an extremely perfumed curry with a pretty green tint. But unless you are a fireeater, you need not use just chili peppers to get the green color. Substitute fresh spinach and coriander or basil leaves.

SERVES 4 PEOPLE

1 **STEAM**
1 frying chicken, about 3 pounds; or 8 thighs or 4 breasts

Place whole chicken on a soup plate and steam in wok over medium-high heat for 20 minutes. If using parts, arrange in a single layer and steam for 15 minutes. Leave chicken to cool.

2 **PUREE**
1 can (4 ounces) green curry paste (Mae Sri)
4 cloves garlic
4 shallots
2 teaspoons shrimp paste
2 to 3 handfuls of basil or coriander leaves, or fresh spinach
5 hot green peppers, seeded and sliced (optional)

Place curry paste, garlic, shallots, and shrimp paste in a mortar or food processor or blender to purée until a paste. (Adding these to the paste will refresh the canned paste.) Blend in the basil or coriander leaves to accentuate the green. Taste the paste and if desired, add hot peppers. Blend well and set aside.

3 **CUT/BONE**
3/4 pound fresh mushrooms

Wipe, then cut mushrooms in half. Take chicken meat off bones and cut or tear into small pieces.

4 **STIR-FRY**
5 tablespoons oil

Heat oil in wok over high heat. When oil is hot, add curry paste and stir-fry until very fragrant, about 2 minutes. Add chicken pieces and mushrooms and turn to coat with sauce.

5 **BRAISE**
2 cups coconut milk

Add coconut milk and bring liquid to boil. Simmer for 10 mintues.

6 **SERVE**
fresh basil leaves

Serve immediately with a great deal of plain rice. Garnish curry with basil leaves.

Turkey Breast and Broccoli Stir-fry

 Turkey breast is easier to slice than chicken breast, since the grain of the meat is larger and easier to ascertain. The broccoli you use in this recipe could be either both the flowerets and stems or just the stems if they are tender and not too thick; the young stems are sweet and crisp, and make a pretty pale green contrast with the turkey.

SERVES 2 PEOPLE

1	**CUT** *½ bunch broccoli*	Peel the broccoli stalks. The fibrous skin runs up the stem and will come off easily if you tear-peel it from the root end up. Cut stems on the diagonal into ⅛- to ¼-inch slices. If using flowerets also, split them lengthwise so the stems are no more than ¼ inch thick.
2	**CUT AND SEASON** *½ pound turkey breast* *2 tablespoons light soy sauce* *1 tablespoon sherry* *1 tablespoon cornstarch*	Slice the turkey breast with the grain into slivers the same size as the broccoli. Combine the soy sauce, sherry, and cornstarch in a bowl. Add turkey and mix well.
3	**STIR-FRY** *2 tablespoons oil* *¼ cup water*	Heat oil in a wok set over high heat. Add the broccoli and toss at a moderate pace until its aroma wafts up to you and it is a dark, bright green, about 2 minutes. Add water and cover for 30 seconds to 1 minute, or until broccoli is tender but still crisp. Scoop out. Wipe wok.
4	**STIR-FRY** *2 tablespoons oil* *1 shallot*	Heat oil in wok over high heat and add shallot. Render in hot oil until it is lightly browned, then discard. Add the turkey and toss until all the pieces have turned white.
5	**COMBINE-FRY**	Add the broccoli and turn to combine with turkey. The juices from the broccoli will thicken the wok liquid very slightly. Serve immediately, with plain rice.

Beef and Peppers

The pre-roasting of the peppers and the addition of the fish sauce are my variations on this traditional dish and perennial favorite.

SERVES 2 TO 4 PEOPLE

1 **CUT AND SEASON**
2 green bell peppers
8 ounces flank steak
2 tablespoons fish
    sauce
1 tablespoon sherry

Seed peppers, and section into 8. Then cut across the lengths for short half-pieces. Peel off membrane of steak with fingers and using the top of a knife if necessary. Cut meat across the grain to the thickness of the pepper slices. Mix fish sauce and sherry, and blend with meat.

2 **DRY-FRY**

Heat a clean, dry wok. Add the peppers and, using a mopping motion with the spatula, press them against the hot steel. The pepper skins will streak brown. Scoop out when the aroma of roasted peppers wafts up to you.

3 **STIR-FRY**
3 tablespoons oil
2 cloves garlic

Pour oil in wok, still over high heat. Add garlic and render, then discard. Toss in the beef and stir-fry, using the fling-and-mop motion until meat has lost its red color, about 2 minutes. Add peppers and serve immediately, with rice.

Beef and Garlic

 This is a dish for the garlic lover—slices of beef in counterpoint with slices of garlic. But use elephant (or large) garlic; its size is amenable to slicing and its flavor mild enough.

SERVES 2 TO 4 PEOPLE

1 **PARBOIL**
1 cup large garlic
   cloves
6 cups water

Cut each garlic into 6 to 8 slices. Bring water to a boil in a saucepan and add the garlic. Boil for 2 minutes, then drain immediately and rinse with cold water until garlic feels cool to the touch.

2 **CUT AND SEASON**
8 ounces flank steak
1 tablespoon soy
   sauce; or 2
   teaspoons dark soy
   and 1 teaspoon
   light soy sauce
1 tablespoon sherry
2 teaspoons sugar
   (optional)

Slice meat across the grain to the same thickness as the garlic slices. Combine soy sauce, sherry, and sugar (if desired), and pour over sliced meat. Mix well.

3 **STIR-FRY**
3 tablespoons oil

Heat oil in wok over high heat. When oil is hot, add the beef and toss vigorously using the mop-and-fling motion. Add the garlic slices when the beef has lost most of its redness, about 2 minutes.

4 **SEASON AND SERVE**
1 tablespoon
   garlic/chili paste,
   approximately
soy sauce
sugar

Add the chili paste and toss. Taste and adjust seasoning—more paste if you like it hotter, soy sauce if you like it saltier, and sugar if you need to quell the attack of the pepper. Serve immediately with a great deal of plain rice; the rice absorbs and erases the residue of spiciness better than a cold liquid.

Wok Beef Stroganoff

Beef stroganoff is no more than stir-fried slices of beef combined with a sauce. Here, butter and flour are turned in the wok to make the brown roux, and the thumbprint noodles from an earlier recipe are cooked right into the sauce. (The noodles absorb the sauce much more successfully this way, are more tender, and the flavors of the entire dish blend better. If you prefer to keep the noodles and meat separate, make the recipe according to the directions but use 2 cups of stock instead of 3.)

SERVES 2 TO 4 PEOPLE

1 **PREPARE** Thumbprint noodle dough; see page 132.

2 **CUT AND SEASON**
1 small onion
2 cloves garlic
3/4 pound flank steak
2 tablespoons brandy or Madeira
3/4 teaspoon salt
black pepper
1 tablespoon red wine vinegar

Dice onion. Crush garlic. Cut steak across the grain into 3-inch strips about 3/8 inch thick. Combine brandy, salt, pepper, and vinegar and pour over the beef. Mix.

3 **HEAT**
3 to 4 cups beef stock

Bring stock to a simmer in a small saucepan. Keep hot.

4 **STIR-FRY**
3 tablespoons clarified butter or oil
4 tablespoons unsalted butter
1/4 cup flour

Heat a wok over high heat and add clarified butter. Stir-fry the beef over high heat until pink, about 3 minutes. Take out. Add unsalted butter and flour and stir-fry over medium heat, turning constantly until the mixture becomes a nutty brown.

5 **COMBINE**
salt and pepper to taste
1 bouquet garni (thyme, bay leaf, parsley)
6 whole cloves
sour cream

Add onion and garlic to wok. They will sizzle as you add them; stir rapidly and when they have stopped sizzling, pour in the stock in 1/2-cup measures, stirring rapidly with the inverted spatula. Add seasonings. Bring liquid to a boil and add the noodles, following directions on page 132. Cover and cook until noodles turn opaque, 5 to 8 minutes. Add meat, stir, and bring to a simmer, and adjust seasonings if necessary. Remove the herbs and cloves. Serve with a twist of the peppermill, and a splash of sour cream if desired.

Beef "Musaman" Curry

 All the Southeast Asian cultures reflect the influences of India and China in their food, but the Thais have taken this most basic Indian classic into a poetic and fragrant world of its own, and prepare it in a Chinese wok. Musaman is Thai for "Moslem," and although most Thai food is among the hottest I've ever eaten, this curry is relatively mild.

SERVES 6 TO 8

1 **ROAST**
1 can (4 ounces) red curry paste (Mai Sri)
5 cloves garlic
5 shallots
2 teaspoons shrimp paste
2 cardamom pods, husks removed
1/2 teaspoon ground cinnamon
1/2 teaspoon ground cloves
5 hot red pepeprs, seeded and sliced (optional)

Preheat oven to 400 degrees. Remove curry paste from can and place on a sheet of aluminum foil along with rest of ingredients. Bake in oven for 15 to 20 minutes until garlic cloves are softened. Pound mixture in a mortar or purée in food processor or blender. Taste paste and, if desired, add hot peppers. Blend until a smooth paste and set aside.

2 **CUT**
2 pounds boneless round or beef chuck

Cut meat into small pieces about 1/4 inch thick.

3 **STIR-FRY**
4 tablespoons oil
1 pound new potatoes
1 pound pearl onions

Heat oil in wok over high heat. When oil is hot, add the meat and stir-fry until it loses its red color, about 2 minutes. Scoop out, leaving oil in wok. Add potatoes and onions. Toss in oil until partially cooked, about 2 minutes, then scoop out. Rinse wok.

4 **STIR-FRY**
3 tablespoons oil

Heat oil in wok over high heat and add curry paste. Turn mixture and stir-fry until fragrant, about 2 minutes.

5 **BRAISE**
4 cups coconut milk
2 teaspoons cider
vinegar (see note)
3 tablespoons brown
sugar (see note)

Add coconut milk, vinegar, and seasonings. Bring to a boil, then add meat and vegetables. Cook, uncovered, until the meat is tender, about 15 to 20 minutes.

6 **SERVE**
fresh basil leaves,
either holy or
purple, or fresh
coriander leaves

Remove mixture from wok and place in serving dish. Garnish with basil or coriander and serve with plenty of plain rice. (The rice is essential for putting out fire in the mouth.)

NOTE: *The vinegar is used in place of the more traditional tamarind water, which is difficult to obtain. If you can get tamarind, knead 3 to 4 seeds in ½ cup of water to obtain 2 teaspoons for the recipe. If you have palm sugar, substitute that for the brown sugar.*

Pork-stuffed Zucchini with Italian Sauce

 SERVES 2 TO 4 PEOPLE

1 **CUT**
3/4 pound small
  zucchini
4 large tomatoes; or
  1 (23-ounce) can
  peeled tomatoes
1 medium onion
2 cloves garlic

Scrub zucchini skins to remove imbedded sand. Cut each in half lengthwise and scrape out seeds. Chop and save these seedy parts. Peel, seed, and dice tomatoes. Dice onion. Mince garlic.

2 **MIX AND STUFF**
1/2 pound ground
  pork (with some
  fat); or 1/2 pound
  Italian sausage
1/2 teaspoon chopped
  fresh basil
1 teaspoon chopped
  fresh parsley
1 clove garlic, minced
1 teaspoon anchovy
  paste
1/4 teaspoon cayenne
salt and pepper

Mix pork, seasonings, and zucchini seed sections. (If using sausage, add only the anchovy paste and cayenne.) Stuff the zucchini halves with the filling, mounding the tops.

3 **FRY**
6 tablespoons olive
  oil

Heat oil in wok over medium heat and then slide the zucchini down the sides of the wok into the hot oil. Nudge them around and splash hot oil over tops. Remove from wok and set aside.

4 **SIMMER**
1 cup white wine
1/4 teaspoon dried
  oregano
1/2 teaspoon chopped
  fresh basil
grated parmesan
  cheese

Add onion and garlic to hot oil in wok over high heat and quickly stir-fry, then add tomatoes and turn the mixture. When it comes to a simmer, add the wine and herbs. Lower zucchini boats back into the wok and scoop some sauce over. Cover and cook over medium heat for 5 minutes or until zucchini are tender and fillings are cooked. Uncover and turn heat to high if the sauce appears a little thin. Transfer zucchini to a serving dish and spoon sauce over. Sprinkle with cheese and serve with pasta, rice, or bread.

Pork and Green Beans with Black Bean Sauce

 It might just be fun to tell your family that you plan to serve pork and beans; then present them with this classic combination of pork stir-fried with green beans, flavored with zesty black beans.

SERVES 2 TO 4 PEOPLE

---

1 **SOAK**
1 tablespoon salted black beans

Rinse beans well and soak in cold water for about 15 minutes. Drain and chop coarsely.

---

2 **CUT**
1/2 pound green beans

Pinch off the stem ends of the beans. Cut each bean with a knife on the diagonal, so they resemble French-cut beans.

---

3 **CUT AND SEASON**
1/2 pound boneless pork
2 teaspoons soy sauce
1 tablespoon sherry
1 tablespoon cornstarch

Remove any membranes from meat and cut across the grain, making long strips the same size as the green beans. In a bowl, mix the soy sauce, sherry, black beans, and cornstarch. Add pork and mix well.

---

4 **STIR-FRY**
1 tablespoon oil
salt to taste

Heat 1 tablespoon oil in wok over high heat. Add green beans and stir steadily. When they have turned a bright green and are cooked throughout, in about 3 to 5 minutes, salt lightly and scoop out. Wipe wok.

---

5 **STIR-FRY**
3 tablespoons oil
1 clove garlic

Heat oil in wok over high heat and render the garlic until it begins to turn brown. Discard. Add the pork and stir-fry, using a mop-and-fling motion.

---

6 **COMBINE-FRY**

When the pork has turned color, add the beans and stir to combine. If the mixture is dry, add a splash of water. Serve immediately with plain rice.

Shortribs Cacciatore

SERVES 4 PEOPLE

1 **MARINATE**
6 to 8 shortribs, each
   6 inches long
6 tablespoons tomato
   paste
1/4 cup red wine
   vinegar
1 tablespoon olive
   oil
1/4 cup minced fresh
   parsley; or 2
   tablespoons dried
1 teaspoon each
   fresh rosemary,
   marjoram, and
   oregano; or 1/2
   teaspoon each
   dried

Place the shortribs in a bowl and add the other ingredients, coating the ribs thoroughly. Let stand while you proceed with rest of recipe.

2 **CUT**
3 medium onions
8 large, ripe
   tomatoes; or 2
   cans (23 ounces)
   whole peeled
   tomatoes
4 bell peppers
4 cloves garlic

Cut onions into eighths. Peel, seed, and coarsely chop the tomatoes. Cut peppers into ¾-inch dice. Mince garlic.

3 **STIR-FRY**
3 tablespoons butter

Melt butter in wok. When the foam almost subsides, add the onions, peppers, and garlic and toss until they wilt, about 3 minutes; remove and set aside. Wipe wok clean.

4 **STIR-FRY**
1/4 cup olive oil

Set wok over high heat and add oil. When oil is hot, add the shortribs and marinade and turn until meat is browned. Add the onions, peppers, garlic, and chopped tomatoes. Turn the mixture a few times to combine.

Thai Chicken
in Green Curry

PAGE *145*

Beef and Garlic

PAGE *148*

Pork-stuffed Zucchini
with Italian Sauce

PAGES 152-153

Scallops
Under Sizzling Herbs

PAGE 163

5 **_STEW_**

2 cups tomato sauce
3 to 4 cups red wine
or beef stock,
approximately

Pour tomato sauce and wine or stock into the wok, adding enough liquid to cover the meat. Cover wok and bring liquid to a boil. Then reduce heat to medium and simmer for about 2 hours. Check every 30 minutes and add stock to just cover the meat. If the liquid reduces too quickly, lower the heat. (Or you can transfer meat to a heavy, straight-sided pan to stew.

6 **_REDUCE_**

When the meat is tender and comes off the bone with a spoon, remove from wok and keep warm. Reduce the sauce by turning the heat to high and letting it boil until most of the liquid is evaporated, about 10 minutes; stir occasionally to keep mixture from sticking. Serve with pasta or rice.

Pork and Fish in Banana Pepper Boats

 The banana-shaped peppers of summer are firm and crisp with a deep aroma. This recipe is best with hot peppers, but substitute the sweet ones if you are timid.

SERVES 4 TO 6 PEOPLE

1 **CUT**
6 banana peppers
½ pound boneless
  pork
¼ pound flounder
  or sole fillets

Halve the peppers and seed them. Separately cut the pork and fish into small pieces. Separately mince them in the food processor or chop by hand. Put both into a small mixing bowl.

2 **SEASON AND STUFF**
1 clove garlic
1 slice gingerroot
1 tablespoon soy
  sauce
1 tablespoon sherry
2 teaspoons oil

Place garlic and ginger in a garlic press and squeeze over the meat and fish. Add soy sauce, sherry, and oil and mix in. If using sweet peppers, you might want to add ½ teaspoon cayenne to the filling for a little fire. Mix well, then using your hands or a spoon, fill pepper shells with the mixture.

3 **FRY**
3 tablespoons oil,
  approximately

Heat oil in wok over high heat. Ease the peppers gently down the sides of wok and drizzle additional oil around if you need more. Nudge the peppers, move them around, and turn over briefly.

4 **SIMMER**
1 tablespoon soy
  sauce
1 tablespoon sherry
2 tablespoons sugar
4 to 6 tablespoons
  water

Add remaining ingredients to wok and use a spatula to spoon the liquid over the peppers. Cover and turn heat to medium high. Cook for 10 to 12 minutes, or until filling is cooked and peppers are crisp but tender. Serve immediately with rice.

Lamb with Turnips and Greens

1 | **CUT**
4 ounces salt pork or bacon
2 pounds boneless lamb

Rinse off the excess salt from the pork or bacon and slice into pieces ⅛ inch thick. Cut the lamb into 1½-inch cubes.

2 | **STIR-FRY**
1 tablespoon oil
1 tablespoon brandy

Heat oil in wok over high heat and add the salt pork. Stir-fry until it has given up some fat, then add the lamb and stir-fry for about 2 minutes. When the meat has lost its red color, add the brandy and toss steadily for 1 minute.

3 | **BRAISE**
4 cups red wine
1 bouquet garni (thyme, bay leaf, rosemary, parsley)
2 teaspoons chopped mint leaves
10 cloves garlic

Add the wine until meat is submerged by 1 inch. Bring to a boil, add the rosemary and mint, and put in the garlic. Cover and simmer on low heat to braise for 2½ to 3½ hours, or until meat is tender. Check every 45 minutes to see if cooking liquid is remaining above the meat; if not, add more wine or water to keep meat covered.

4 | **ADD**
4 small to medium turnips, peeled and quartered
1 pound turnip greens or spinach, trimmed

About 1 hour before serving, add turnips, making sure they are surrounded by cooking liquid. If necessary, add more wine or water to bring up level. When turnips are tender and have turned opaque, after about 50 minutes, use a perforated ladle to move meat and turnips to a serving dish. Bring gravy in wok to a boil. Add turnip greens and cover. Cook until tender but still crisp, about 2 minutes. Remove greens with the perforated ladle and place on a separate serving dish. Bring liquid in wok back to a boil and, over high heat, boil until reduced to about 1½ cups.

5 | **SEASON AND SERVE**
1 tablespoon anchovy or tomato paste
2 tablespoons butter
salt and pepper

Strain cooking liquid and pull out garlic cloves; the skins will come off easily. With a fork, quickly mash the garlic in a small bowl along with the anchovy paste and butter. Fold this paste into the sauce, season to taste, and spoon a little over vegetables. Pour the rest over the meat. Serve with rice or buttered noodles, or with good fresh bread.

Lamb and Eggplant with Garlic Sauce

1 **CUT**
3/4 pound small or "oriental" eggplant
1 pound boneless lamb shoulder or breast; or ground lamb
2 leeks
4 cloves garlic
1 cup packed fresh Italian parsley
1 ripe, medium tomato

Cut eggplant into ⅝-inch sticks. Slice the lamb and mince by hand or by machine. Mince the leeks and garlic. Mince parsley. Peel, seed and dice tomato.

2 **SEASON**
¼ cup tomato paste
1 tablespoon sherry

Place the lamb in a bowl and add tomato paste and sherry. Blend well.

3 **STIR-FRY**
6 to 8 tablespoons olive oil, approximately

Place wok over high heat. When the wok is hot, pour in oil and let it become very hot. Add the eggplant and toss until it is soft, about 5 minutes. You may need to add more oil because some types of eggplant are more absorbent. As the eggplant cooks, it will become soft and translucent. At this point, it will release some excess oil. Press with the back of the spatula to squeeze out more, then remove the eggplant and leave the residual oil. (Do not wipe wok.)

4 **STIR-FRY**
1 tablespoon olive oil, approximately

Add enough oil to that left in the wok to make 2 tablespoons, then add leeks, parsley, and garlic. Toss until soft, about 2 minutes, then add lamb and turn the mixture until the lamb has turned color.

5 **COMBINE-FRY**
2 bay leaves
1 teaspoon chopped
   fresh mint
1/2 teaspoon dried
   oregano
1/4 teaspoon dried
   rosemary
1/3 cup beef or lamb
   stock
1 to 2 tablespoons
   garlic-chili paste
Salt and pepper to
   taste

Return the eggplant to the wok and add herbs. Turn the mixture to combine. Pour in the stock and continue to turn the mixture over high heat until liquid has been absorbed. Then fold in garlic-chili paste. Adjust seasoning with salt and pepper, and more garlic-chili paste, if desired.

6 **SERVE**

Remove the bay leaves. Sprinkle the diced tomatoes over the mixture and serve immediately with bread, pasta, or rice.

Tofu and Bean Sprouts with Spicy Peanut Sauce

 Indonesians infuse things Chinese with their blend of the sweet and spicy. Here they simmer bean curd and bean sprouts with their favored red peppers and peanuts. Peanut butter is used in place of deep-fried ground peanuts to facilitate the preparation.

SERVES 4 PEOPLE

1 **WASH AND SOAK**
½ pound bean sprouts
1 pound tofu

Rinse sprouts in a sinkful of water. Swish them with your hand to separate out the hulls and stray roots. Lift the sprouts into a colander and leave roots and hulls in sink. Place tofu in a large bowl of water.

2 **PUREE**
1 fresh cayenne pepper or to taste
2 teaspoons shrimp paste
2 cloves garlic
2 shallots

Seed and slice pepper into thin slices. Place pepper with remaining ingredients into a food processor or mortar and blend or pound until you have a rough paste.

3 **STIR-FRY**
3 tablespoons oil
salt

Heat oil in a wok over high heat. When oil is hot, add sprouts. Toss moderately, then add salt and stir steadily for 4 minutes. Scoop out. Wipe wok.

4 **STIR-FRY**
2 tablespoons oil

Heat oil in wok over high heat, then ease the block of tofu down the wall of the wok. Use the tip of the spatula and cut block into 4 slices. Spread slices out gently, then fry on both sides. There will be a slight crumbling of the tofu but do not handle it too much or it will break up completely. Stir-fry for 3 minutes, then remove.

5 **COMBINE-FRY**
2 tablespoons oil
⅓ cup peanut butter, preferably natural
2 tablespoons dark soy sauce
2 teaspoons sugar
¾ cup coconut milk or water

Heat oil in wok over high heat. When oil is hot, pour in the paste and turn until its aroma wafts up to your nose. Add peanut butter and remaining seasonings. (If you have had to use pre-sweetened peanut butter, eliminate the sugar.) When sauce begins to simmer, pour in the tofu and coconut milk. Turn mixture gently, cover, and let sauce simmer for several minutes to allow flavors to penetrate tofu. Add the bean sprouts and give the mixture a few gentle turns. Then scoop out mixture into a dish—tofu first—and top with sprouts and cooking liquid. Serve with plain rice.

Dressy Food

This chapter features dishes which are more inclined for special occasions. Either the recipes are more challenging or the ingredients more costly—in other words, foods that make you feel dressed up. The preparations involved vary enormously, offering a range of techniques depending on your particular demands and needs. For instance, the Smothered Veal and the Lobster on a Bed of Basil are cooked in a matter of minutes, whereas the Red Chicken and the Chicken and Whole Pesto involve more complex steps that take a bit longer. Depending on what other dishes you are serving, and your experience with the wok, you should choose recipes that you can prepare with ease for your company.

Don't be deterred by recipes in this chapter which indicate a small number of servings. These can easily be made to feed larger parties with just minor adjustments. The recipes are in smaller form in this book because optimum use of the wok generally means cooking in small quantities. When entertaining involves cooking for more than 2 or 4, you can accommodate the increase in either of two ways: by adjusting your menu so the dish is part of a larger selection of dishes, or by adjusting the procedure when you begin to cook the recipe. For the latter option, here are some tips:

Cut, wash, season, and do all the other preparations ahead of stir-frying, using doubled measurements.

Separate and stir-fry ingredients into two portions to match the original recipe, and separately stir-fry each portion.

At the combine-fry step, combine all your ingredients for a quick re-heating.

For example, if you were to double the quantity for Lobster Chinoise, just prepare twice the number of ingredients and double-up on every procedure except the stir-fry for the lobster. Separately stir-fry the portions of lobster (the first batch will not cool down very much while you stir-fry the second batch). Then cook the sauce ingredients in double quantity, and finally incorporate the two lobster portions into the sauce for a final quick combining and re-heating.

Similarly for steaming in quantity, you can stack bamboo steamers in the wok and steam the portions all together after you have prepared and seasoned the double portions.

These recipes are largely main dishes, but you can offer your guests multiple "main" courses, even serve a number of small courses. If you select a recipe from this chapter and wish to accompany it with another "main" course, make your selection one hot dish and one cold or one that does not require elaborate preparation, or that can be reheated. This way, entertaining will be easier for you, and you'll please your guests with the variety of your table.

Scallops Under Sizzling Herbs

A tousled head of curly fresh herbs sits atop these quickly steamed scallops. The herbs are showered at the table with hot olive oil, and they sizzle and curl as the fragrant oil rains down through the scallops. Only very tender herbs must be used. Scrape them aside after sizzling or serve and eat them with the scallops as a type of warm salad. Watercress and parsley make good eating, but use discretion with the red pepper and other herbs.

SERVES 4 PEOPLE

---

1 **TRIM AND FLOAT**
1 bunch flat-leaf
   parsley or
   watercress
1 small pinch fresh
   oregano or
   marjoram
2 scallions
1 bunch chives
1 fresh hot red
   pepper
1 clove garlic

Pinch off only young tips of the parsley and oregano or marjoram; you should have about 1 cup of leaves. Use only the white parts of the scallions and split them lengthwise. Use the lower 1 inch of the chives (the white part) and cut up; you should have ¼ cup. Seed and sliver the red pepper. Slice the garlic thinly. Float all the herbs in a bowl of cold water with a few ice cubes. If slivered fine enough, they will curl.

---

2 **COMBINE**
1 pound scallops
¼ teaspoon salt
1 tablespoon
   Madeira

Mix scallops with salt and wine in steaming dish.

---

3 **STEAM**

Bring water to a boil in a wok, with rack in place. Add dish with scallops and steam over high heat for 3 to 5 minutes.

---

4 **HEAT**
⅓ cup olive oil
¼ teaspoon salt

While scallops steam, heat oil and salt in a saucepan until oil almost smokes.

---

5 **SERVE**

Drain herbs and as soon as scallops are firm to the touch, lift steaming plate out of wok onto serving platter. Amass herbs over scallops and bring to the table along with hot oil. Pour hot oil over herbs. Toss lightly after they have sizzled, and serve with rice or bread.

Whole "Roasted" Shrimp

The shrimp are not really "roasted." They are plunged three times into explosively hot oil, and pulled out quickly before the oil cools; at no time does the shrimp cook in oil that is trying to reheat itself. The shrimp shells act as the natural protective coating. It is a simple, stunning treatment especially if you have fresh whole shrimp with their heads on. These shrimp are peeled at the table and have a certain casual elegance because they taste so smooth and suave—quite different from boiled shrimp.

For this recipe, you'll need a wire basket or large scoop. The shrimp must not be layered more than 2 deep in the basket, and each dunking must completely immerse the contents of the basket, too, so don't skimp on the oil either. Finish the dish by stir-frying the shrimp with one of two flavorings and serve with your finger bowls of tea or lemon water.

SERVES 4 PEOPLE

---

1 **TRIM**
1 pound large shrimp with heads, or about 1½ pounds headed

Wash shrimp. If using whole shrimp, use a kitchen shears to cut off ¼ inch tips from heads in order to remove the 2 sharp protrusions and long antennae.

---

2 **DRY**

Towel dry shrimp thoroughly, then wrap a towel around the shrimp and wring it gently. Spread out shrimp on another dry towel to air dry. (The drying is very important; moisture left on shrimp will explode in deep fat.)

---

3 **DEEP-FRY**
4 cups oil

Bring oil in wok to 375 degrees. Arrange shrimp in wire basket, in one or 2 layers only; all shrimp should fit into basket, but stacking shrimp will minimize the effect of the heat and retard cooking. Immerse basket in hot oil and count 8 seconds, then lift the basket out. Count 15 seconds while oil reheats and moisture evaporates. (You will see steam and air bubbles rising from oil.) Dunk a second time and count 5 seconds, then haul shrimp and wait another 15-second interval. Dunk a third time for 5 seconds, then put shrimp aside. Pour hot oil into a metal container, straining it if you wish. Leave 1½ tablespoons of oil in wok.

WITH GINGER AND SCALLIONS

4 **STIR-FRY**
*2 scallions, cut in
  2-inch sections
2 slices gingerroot,
  ¹/₈ inch thick
salt
2 teaspoons sherry*

Add scallions and ginger to oil left in wok and stir-fry for 2 minutes. When aroma is released, add the shrimp and sherry. Stir-fry until wine evaporates. Season to taste with salt and serve immediately.

WITH OREGANO OR THYME

4 **STIR-FRY**
*8 leaves fresh
  oregano or thyme
salt
1¹/₂ teaspoons wine
  vinegar*

Add herb to wok and stir-fry until the aroma is released, about 2 minutes. Add shrimp and vinegar and stir-fry until vinegar has evaporated. Add salt to taste and serve immediately.

Lobster Chinoise

This lobster must be killed and stir-fried, not boiled first, to best retain the fresh and sweet taste of the meat. As the pieces of lobster are stir-fried, the juices caught between the shell and the flesh go into the buttery stir-fry mixture of pork, capers, tomato paste, Madeira, and tarragon. Then an egg is stirred in at the last minute to bind all these good things, including loose flakes of lobster meat, roe, and juices. It becomes a sauce of body and substance, which my father prefers to the actual lobster.

Have courage. It hurts the lobster no more to kill it in this way than to boil it. A sharp cleaver easily cuts through the shell. Choose a lively lobster, but chill it for an hour or so; a cold lobster is sleepy, and easier to handle. Then put on gloves or oven mitts and immediately cut off the claws, severing them at the joints touching the body; they will come off easily. Now insert a sharp knife under the shell of the head segment and sever the nerve. The lobster will be dead; any squirms you see are residual reflexes. Remove the legs and split the head down the middle lengthwise. Remove the sac and intestines. Cut the tail through the shell into segments 1 inch long, or follow the natural segmentations. Separate the second joints from the claws and crack the claws and second joints using the flat side of a cleaver or a nut cracker, but do not peel off the shells. This way the flavors will penetrate the jagged fractures in the shell but protect the flesh from direct heat. Store cut pieces on a serving platter, covered with a damp cloth, and chill in refrigerator for up to 6 hours before cooking.*

SERVES 2 AS A MAIN COURSE

---

1 | **DRESS**
1 lobster, 1½ pounds | Prepare lobster, following instructions given above.

---

2 | **MINCE**
2 cloves garlic
¼ pound boneless pork, or ¼ pound ground pork
1 bunch scallions | Mince garlic into fine bits. Cut meat into thin slices and mince in food processor or by hand. Cut scallions into thin rounds, keeping green parts separate to use as a garnish later.

---

3 | **STIR-FRY**
2 tablespoons olive oil
2 tablespoons butter
1 teaspoon capers | Heat olive oil and butter in wok until butter has foamed, then subsided. Stir-fry the garlic, scallion whites, and capers over high heat. When the scallions become limp, add the meat. Toss and stir vigorously, inverting the spatula to break up the meat. When the meat turns white, add the lobster pieces. Turn pieces until the shells become hard red, about 5 minutes.

4 **_SEASON AND BIND_**
¼ cup Madeira
1 tablespoon tomato
*   paste*
⅛ teaspoon cayenne
¼ teaspoon
*   tarragon*
salt and pepper
2 eggs, stirred

Add seasonings to wok and toss. Continue to toss until mixture bubbles. Pour eggs over the lobster, count to 5, and then turn the mixture with the spatula a few times until the eggs are just set. Scoop out immediately and serve with rice or bread. Garnish with minced scallion greens. Have a spoon handy to collect the sauce mixture.

*Improvisation not recommended; use all measurements as given.

Lobster on a Bed of Basil

This recipe is a lean treatment for lobster, suggested by a Thai recipe for crab steamed with holy basil. The three dipping sauces are easy to make and can be prepared hours in advance. But don't let the fragrance and natural simplicity of the dish be overpowered by the hot pepper in the sauce; add the pepper to suit your tolerance.

Choose the fiestiest, most athletic lobster. Once home, refrigerate it to slow it down, then follow the instructions in the previous recipe to dress it or have your fishmonger do it for you. If you want to serve 1 lobster per person, do not section the tail, nor cut off the head. Just split the lobster whole from the head to the tail on the underside and press it open. When steaming, place the lobsters side by side on the plate with the cut sides up so the steam can work directly on the exposed flesh.

SERVES 2 PEOPLE

1

DRESS
1 lobster, about 1 to
1½ pounds

Follow directions in the previous recipe.

2

STEAM
8 long branches fresh
holy basil, or
purple or sweet
basil
2 slices gingerroot,
slivered
2 tablespoons sherry

Bring water in wok to a boil over high heat. Arrange a bed of 4 basil branches on a steaming plate and sprinkle on half the ginger slivers. Lay the lobster pieces on the bed and drizzle with the sherry. Blanket the lobster with the remaining basil and sprinkle with remaining ginger slivers. Cover and steam over high heat for 10 to 15 minutes.

3

PREPARE SAUCES

**Lime and Chili
Pepper Dip**
juice of 1 lime
1½ teaspoons sugar
¼ cup fish sauce
1 fresh hot red or
green pepper

Stir together the lime juice, sugar, and fish sauce until sugar melts. Seed and slice the pepper into thin rounds, then float the rounds on the dip.

**Garlic and Chili
Dip**
2 cloves garlic
1 hot red pepper,
seeded
1 to 4 teaspoons
water

In a mortar, pound the garlic with the pepper until a paste or push together through a garlic press. Work in water, 1 teaspoon at a time, until mixture is a sauce.

Hot Pepper Sauce
1 fresh hot green
  pepper
fish sauce

Core and slice pepper into rounds. Place in a small bowl and barely cover with fish sauce.

4 **SERVE**

Lift the plate onto a larger platter and serve lobster steaming hot with dipping sauces on the side. The basil and ginger are a garnish, not meant to be eaten.

Scallops Maison

This is the favorite way of enjoying scallops in my home. The scallops are combined with pieces of pork and cucumbers, and the cucumbers—because they have a glaze on them—shimmer with a jadelike softness that is like the white of the scallops. If pressed for time, the cucumbers and pork may be cooked ahead of time, with the final stir-fry at the last minute.

SERVES 4 PEOPLE

---

1 | **DICE**
1 long cucumber, or
   2 smaller | Peel and seed the cucumber. Cut into ½-inch cubes.

---

2 | **COOK**
2 tablespoons sugar
6 tablespoons
   unsalted butter
pinch of salt | Combine sugar, butter, and salt in a small saucepan with the cucumber. Add water to ¾ way up the cucumbers. Bring to a boil and cook over medium high heat until the liquid is almost all evaporated and a shiny glaze coats the cucumbers, about 15 minutes.

---

3 | **CUT MEAT**
8 ounces boneless
   pork tenderloin
2 teaspoons Madeira
1 teaspoon
   cornstarch
1 teaspoon oil
salt and pepper | Cut meat into ½-inch cubes. Pour seasonings into diced pork and mix. (You may stir-fry it at this stage and set it aside.)

---

4 | **SEASON SCALLOPS**
1 pound bay scallops
2 teaspoons Madeira
1 tablespoon
   cornstarch
¼ teaspoon white
   pepper | Mix scallops with seasonings and set aside.

---

5 | **STIR-FRY**
2 tablespoons oil
1 clove garlic | Heat oil in wok over high heat. Add garlic, render, and then discard when it turns brown. Add pork and toss at moderate pace for 2 minutes. Scoop out. Rinse wok.

---

6 | **STIR-FRY**
2 tablespoons oil | About 10 minutes before serving, heat oil in wok over high heat. Stir-fry the scallops for 30 seconds. Add the cooked pork, then toss to combine and re-heat the meat. Add the cucumbers and turn mixture gently. When ingredients are thoroughly heated, serve over rice or noodles.

Salmon in Bombay Gin

PAGES 176-177

Whole Crispy Game Hens

PAGES *188-189*

Crabmeat Over Tofu

Tofu can be a pedestrian ingredient, but when combined with crabmeat, its regal face shows with a delicacy and subtlety that matches that of crabmeat. Moreover, it absorbs the flavors and juices of the crab, lending finesse with its smooth texture. For this dish, use only soft tofu, and preferably a good sake or Chinese rice wine.*

SERVES 2 TO 4 PEOPLE

---

1   **SOAK**
1 pound soft tofu

Place tofu in a bowl of fresh water to cover and allow to soak while you prepare dish.

---

2   **MIX**
1½ tablespoons cornstarch
½ cup chicken stock
1 tablespoon sake or sherry
¼ teaspoon salt

Stir cornstarch with remaining ingredients and set aside.

---

3   **FRY**
2 tablespoons oil
½ teaspoon salt

Heat oil in a wok over medium high heat and ease tofu into the oil. Cut tofu into 6 slices using the tip of the spatula, then gently spread pieces out in wok. Add salt and turn and fry tofu on both sides for about 2 minutes. A little shattering will take place, but you should end up with spoon-sized pieces. Scoop out gently and set aside.

---

4   **STIR-FRY**
2 tablespoons oil
1 scallion, cut in 2-inch sections
1 slice gingerroot, ⅛ inch thick
1 cup lump crabmeat

Heat oil in wok and render scallion and ginger over medium-high heat. When the aromas rise up to your nose, discard both. Turn the heat to medium and add the crabmeat to wok, tossing for a few seconds. Quickly re-stir the cornstarch mixture and immediately pour over the crabmeat. Turn steadily but gently until the sauce thickens and becomes translucent.

---

5   **COMBINE-FRY**

Add tofu carefully, letting it slide down the wok wall. Adjust the heat to high, and turn and fold the mixture until it bubbles, about 3 minutes.

---

6   **SERVE**
white pepper
minced scallion greens
steamed Belgian endive leaves

Scoop mixture into a serving bowl and sprinkle with white pepper. Garnish with minced greens or over an arrangement of lightly steamed endive. Serve with rice.

---

*Improvisation not recommended; use all measurements as given.

Steamed Trout with Cream Sauce

In this recipe, trout is topped with pieces of shrimp and steamed with potatoes. You make the sauce while the fish is steaming, and both are ready in 25 minutes. The trick is to have the sauce and fish ready at the same time. Once you start cooking, you will move from step to step without stopping, but also without scurrying.

SERVES 2 PEOPLE

1 | **PEEL**
6 to 10 new or red potatoes; or ½ pound Idaho potatoes | Peel potatoes, then cut new potatoes in half and larger potatoes in slices ⅜ inch thick. Arrange potatoes on one side of a steaming plate.

2 | **STEAM** | Boil water in wok, with rack in place. Add the plate with the potatoes, and steam for 10 minutes.

3 | **REDUCE**
1½ cups heavy cream
¼ teaspoon salt
pinch of black pepper
1 shallot, crushed | While potatoes are steaming, place ingredients in a small saucepan and boil until reduced to ¾ cup. Leave on the burner to cool slightly.

4 | **STEAM**
2 trout fillets, each 8 to 12 ounces
¼ cup peeled and deveined small shrimp | Insert a knife into the potatoes; they should be almost done. Put the fish on the plate with the potatoes and arrange shrimp on top of them. Cover and steam for 3 to 5 minutes.

5 | **ENRICH**
2 egg yolks
6 to 10 drops fish sauce
1 teaspoon lemon juice | When sauce is no longer hot but warm, whisk in the egg yolks rapidly. Add fish sauce and lemon juice, then remove shallot and discard.

6 | **SERVE**
minced fresh parsley | Check fish in steamer and cook a little longer if not quite done. As soon as it is cooked, remove from steamer and pour sauce over fish. Sprinkle potatoes with parsley, then lift dish onto a larger plate and serve immediately.

Steamed Sole Vinaigrette

In this recipe, the sole rests on an attractive sheet of green spinach, and both are steamed together. When you serve, you'll have the vegetable and fish in one, all dressed with vinaigrette—in 20 minutes total. A thin salmon steak is also pretty, with the green spinach in the background.

SERVES 2 PEOPLE

---

1 **PREPARE**
1½ to 2-pound sole, dressed, or 2 sole fillets
3 scallions, cut in 2-inch sections
3 slices gingerroot
¼ cup sherry

Check fish for stray scales. Rinse out cavity and pat dry. Score both sides of the fish on the diagonal and with the knife tilted close to horizontal. Make 2 to 3 slashes (you need not score the fillets). Bruise scallion sections and ginger slices with a knife blade and then combine with sherry in a bowl. Bathe the fish with this alcohol rub, especially the cavity.

---

2 **ASSEMBLE**
8 to 12 young whole spinach leaves, washed

Shake excess moisture off leaves. Make a bed of spinach leaves around the center of a steaming dish. Place fish over the spinach leaves in the steaming plate.

---

3 **STEAM**

Bring water to a boil in a wok, with rack in place. Steam fish over high heat for about 7 minutes, then check to see if it is done. If not, continue to steam for an additional 3 to 4 minutes. Do not overcook.

---

4 **MIX**
⅓ cup olive oil
1½ tablespoons wine vinegar
salt and pepper
1 clove garlic, minced
2 teaspoons Dijon-style mustard
1 teaspoon Worcestershire sauce

While fish is steaming, combine dressing ingredients in a bottle and shake thoroughly. Place bottle in a small saucepan with hot water to gently heat the vinaigrette. Serve fish as soon as it is done, lifting steaming dish off of the rack and placing it on another platter. Pour dressing over and serve. Have plenty of good bread on hand.

Poached Trout with Sweet and Sour Sauce

 *A poached freshwater fish is more subtle and demands a mellower sweet and sour sauce than the deep-fried version, so it is made with the brown Zijiang vinegar, which is a very soft, earthy and aromatic rice vinegar.**

SERVES 4 PEOPLE

---

1 **SEASON**
2 large trout,
  cleaned
2 scallions
4 slices gingerroot,
  each ⅛ inch thick
½ cup rice wine,
  sake or sherry

Cut scallions into 2-inch segments. Place in a dish along with the wine. Lightly crush the scallion and ginger with the handle of a knife to release their juices, then add the fish, turning and bathing it in the mixture. Rub some of the seasoning into the cavity, too. Cover fish with plastic wrap and refrigerate for 30 minutes.

---

2 **POACH**
6 cups water

Cover and bring water to a vigorous boil in the wok over high heat. Slide in one fish and let water come to a simmer. Use the ladle to scoop and continuously splash water onto the exposed parts. Cook for about 3 minutes after the water has returned to a boil, and turn the fish once. When the fish eyes have turned white, fish is done, in about 5 minutes. Insert a paring knife into the thickest part of the fish, near the head. If there is no pink near the bone and the flesh separates easily, remove fish from the wok with a perforated spatula and place in a warmed serving dish. Poach the second fish.

---

3 **MIX**
1½ cups chicken
  stock
¼ cup Zijiang
  vinegar
3 tablespoons sugar
2 tablespoons soy
  sauce
1 tablespoon sherry
2 teaspoons salt
3 tablespoons
  cornstarch mixed
  with 3 tablespoons
  water

Place ingredients for sauce in wok and bring to a boil over high heat. Pour cornstarch mixture into sauce and stir constantly until sauce thickens and bubbles, turning opaque.

4 **SERVE**
   1 tablespoon sesame oil
   1 tablespoon oil
   2 slices gingerroot, cut in 2-inch shreds (optional)
   1 scallion, cut in shreds (optional)

Pour the oils into the wok and turn 2 or 3 times with the spatula. Scoop the sauce out and onto the fish. Serve with thin shreds of ginger and scallion, if desired.

*Improvisation not recommended; use all measurements as given.

Salmon in Bombay Gin

This salmon is bathed in gin, then steamed and served cold with three colorful sauces. Bombay gin is a dizzingly aromatic gin, but you could use another brand with almost as good results.*

SERVES 6 PEOPLE

---

1 **CUT**
1 small whole salmon, about 3 to 4 pounds; or 6 salmon steaks, cut 1 inch thick

Split the fish in half lengthwise, using a sharp boning knife. If the head is still on, split that in half lengthwise too, using a cleaver. One half of the fish will have the tail and the back bone; the other will not. Leave the skin on; this is a natural fatty layer that automatically bastes the fish as it cooks.

---

2 **MARINATE**
½ cup gin, preferably Bombay

Baste the flesh of each side of the fish with the gin, using a brush. The fish will absorb all the gin. Leave fish at room temperature for 1 hour.

---

3 **STEAM**

Bring water in wok to a boil, with rack in place. Place fish halves skin side up in a steaming dish. (The dish need not contain the entire fish; the ends can hang out.) Steam over high heat for 10 minutes, then test the thickest part of the fish. If it comes off the bone easily and there is no pink, it is done. Let cool.

---

4 **SEASON**
¼ cup olive oil
2 teaspoons salt

While fish is steaming, heat oil in a small saucepan and add salt. As soon as the salt is dissolved, let oil cool. When fish has cooled and become firm enough to handle, invert dish onto a flat platter and lift off entire backbone, if using whole salmon. Brush flesh with the oil mixture and refrigerate for at least 2 hours.

---

5 **PREPARE SAUCE**

Avocado Sauce
1 avocado
½ cup yoghurt
1 cup chopped watercress
½ teaspoon lime juice
salt and pepper

Place ingredients into the bowl of a food processor or blender and whirl until smooth. There will be bright green flecks of watercress in the purée.

Curry Sauce

2 tablespoons curry
  powder
2 teaspoons cayenne
3 tablespoons water
1/2 medium onion
1 clove garlic
1 cup coconut milk,
  preferably
  unsweetened
1 teaspoon vinegar
salt and pepper

Mix together in a small bowl, the curry powder, cayenne, and water. The curry powder will absorb all the liquid. Blend together the onion, garlic, coconut milk, vinegar, and salt and pepper in the bowl of a food processor or blender. Add the curry paste and blend well.

Gin Vinaigrette

1 ounce (2
  tablespoons) gin,
  preferably Bombay
2 ounces (1/4 cup)
  tonic water
1/2 teaspoon lime
  juice
1/2 cup buttermilk
salt and pepper
1/2 teaspoon juniper
  berries

Mix ingredients in a bottle or in a small bowl, using a whisk. Float the juniper berries on top.

6 **SERVE**
watercress sprigs
lemon slices

Serve fish with all the 3 sauces, or just 1. The whole fish may be presented on a large platter, butterfly-style, or the 2 halves separated onto 2 platters and placed on 2 sides of a large table. Garnish with watercress and lemon.

*Improvisation not recommended; use all measurements as given.

Carved Squash Soup

A clear soup with cubes of chicken or ham and mushrooms is cooked inside a winter squash or pumpkin. The presentation is dramatic and the carving fun. I use an abstract design, but whatever you choose, do not carve through the meat of the squash; merely etch out a design on the skin.

The squash and soup are steamed together, with the shell of the squash forming a perfect container for cooking the soup in the fashion of a double boiler or bain-marie. Serve the soup by bringing the squash to the table and ladling out the aromatic, clear soup. This does not taste assertively "squash," or "pumpkin," rather it is fresh-perfumed by the delicate hint of steamed squash.

Pumpkins and winter squashes come to harvest in the early fall. You can use any round squash which will stand stable on its bottom, but a green pumpkin is especially striking. Find a ceramic or heatproof bowl (it should be unobtrusive, closer to a saucer) to hold the squash, lightly cupping the bottom to give it additional support and allow you to transport the squash to the table after it is soft from cooking. If you intend to use a very large squash, you'll have to improvise a steamer larger than your wok, but a stockpot will suffice. You don't need a rack; the bowl which holds the squash can sit directly in the water and the water should come halfway up the bowl.

SERVES 6 TO 8 PEOPLE

---

1 **CARVE**
1 round winter
　squash or green
　pumpkin, about
　16 inches around

Cut off and discard top ¼ of squash. Hollow out, leaving a ¾-inch wall. Use a knife with a sharp point to cut your design into the skin only. Place squash in steaming dish and then place dish into wok for steaming. Make sure squash fits under the wok lid with room for steam to move about. If not, try lowering the rack or trimming off more of the top. Check that you have enough water or stock to fill the hollowed-out squash up to within 1 inch of the rim.

---

2 **BOIL**
4 cups chicken stock
　or water,
　approximately
1 whole chicken
　breast, boned,
　skinned, and meat
　cut into ½-inch
　dice
1 cup diced fresh
　mushrooms
½ cup diced boiled
　ham

Place water or stock in a saucepan and bring to a boil. Add the chicken, mushrooms, and ham. Simmer for 15 to 20 minutes.

3 *STEAM*

Bring water in wok to a simmer, with rack in place. Put squash into supporting bowl and place bowl onto steaming rack. Pour the simmering soup into the squash and cover wok. Steam over medium-low heat for about 40 minutes—it should not cook so long as to droop. Add boiling water to wok when necessary to keep up level. When squash is finished steaming, bring to table in steaming saucer. Ladle soup directly out of the mouth of the squash.

Veal and Sweet Basil

Though the original inspiration for this dish is the Thai recipe Beef and Basil (page 74), this version is a veal cutlet fried with the more common sweet basil leaves and sauced with garlic and a touch of anchovy paste, more properly a new Italian recipe. It can also be made with center-cut pork chops.*

SERVES 4 PEOPLE

---

1   **PUREE**
4 cloves garlic
4 shallots
1 tablespoon
   anchovy paste
1 tablespoon
   Marsala wine

Blend garlic, shallots, and anchovy paste in a mortar or a blender until you have a smooth paste. Add the wine and mix well.

---

2   **TRIM**
1 bunch fresh sweet
   basil

Pinch off leaves and clusters, discarding stalks and tougher branches. You should have 2 cups of leaves. Wash and drain.

---

3   **SLICE AND SEASON**
4 veal chops cut
   1/4-inch thick,
   about 1 pound

Cut the meat from the bone. Pound briefly between pieces of waxed paper to thin them as much as possible. Place cutlets in a bowl and add the paste. Mix well.

---

4   **STIR-FRY**
1/4 cup oil
1/4 cup slivered
   almonds
2 cloves garlic, sliced
   thin

Heat oil in wok over high heat, then add almonds. Stir-fry until they take on a toasty gold coloring, about 1 minute. Remove and set aside. In same oil, fry the garlic slices until brown, then remove and drain on a paper towel. Add the veal to the oil and turn once or twice until cooked, about 3 minutes.

---

5   **SEASON**
1 tablespoon olive
   oil
2 tablespoons
   Marsala wine
few drops lemon
   juice

When meat is almost done, pull the slices up the sides of the wok. Add the basil leaves to the remaining oil in the center of the wok and stir-fry, tossing steadily. Drizzle in the olive oil to give extra fragrance. Once the leaves start to wilt, 2 or 3 seconds, push down the meat, splash with the wine, and cover wok for 1 minute. Uncover and squeeze in a few drops of lemon juice. Serve with rice or pasta, sprinkled with the almonds and garlic chips.

---

*Improvisation not recommended; use all measurements as given.

Smothered Veal Chops

Scallions cook to a mellow sweetness much faster than bulb onions or leeks, and they claim an individual taste. This variation on a favorite can also be made with pork chops with equal success.

SERVES 2 PEOPLE

1 **WASH AND TRIM**
2 bunches scallions

Cut scallions into 2-inch sections. Do not cut higher than 6 inches from the root ends; the upper parts are tough. Rinse and dry.

2 **FRY**
1/4 cup oil,
approximately
2 loin veal chops

Heat oil in wok over high heat. When hot, slide in the chops. Brown on both sides, nudging them once in a while to prevent sticking. Cook for about 15 minutes, depending on the thickness of the chops. Push chops up the side of the wok, clearing the center. Add the scallions and toss until they wilt. Drizzle in additional oil, if necessary, to keep scallions from sticking.

3 **SEASON AND DEGLAZE**
2 tablespoons brandy
salt and pepper
1/3 cup white wine or
stock

Pour brandy into wok and season with salt and pepper. Push chops back into center of wok and turn the mixture a few times. Add wine or stock to dissolve and loosen the meat particles attached to wok bottom, forming a light, natural sauce. Cover wok and turn down heat to let mixture cook for 2 to 3 minutes, or until chops are done. Test chops and serve with noodles or rice.

Veal Roulades with Orange Peel

 *Very thin slices of veal (or substitute beef or pork) are rolled around a candied orange peel, then braised in an orange sauce. The strips of almost-burnt orange peel flavor the oil and are not meant to be consumed, but do retain them for a garnish.**

SERVES 4 PEOPLE

---

1 | **PEEL AND DRY**
1 orange | Score the orange into quarters, then peel. Cut and scrape away most of the pith and membranes. Sliver each quarter into thin strips and leave out to dry overnight.

---

2 | **SLICE AND MARINATE**
1 pound veal loin
1/4 cup soy sauce
1 tablespoon sherry
1/8 teaspoon tarragon | Use a sharp knife to shave off thin slices of meat; you should get about 12 thin slices. Pound slices briefly between sheets of waxed paper, using the flat side of a cleaver, then set slices into a bowl. Pour soy sauce, sherry, and tarragon over and let marinate for 5 minutes.

---

3 | **ASSEMBLE**
1/4 pound candied orange peel
1/4 cup cornstarch | Take veal out a slice at a time and roll each slice loosely around a stick of orange peel. Dust lightly with the cornstarch. If the meat has been sliced very thin, it will stay rolled around the peel; if you are unsure, fasten each roulade with a toothpick. You will have about 1 tablespoon of marinade left in the bowl.

---

4 | **DEEP-FRY**
2 cups oil | Heat oil in wok until 350 degrees. Fry the roulades 3 at a time for about 10 seconds each. Lift out with a perforated ladle and return to the marinade. Continue to deep-fry remaining roulades, then place them back into marinade. Pour off oil in wok, retaining about 3 tablespoons; there will be some sediment in wok from the loose cornstarch—that's all right.

---

5 | **STIR-FRY** | Return wok to heat and drop in dried peel. Cook to render the aroma and oils from the peel and when peel turns very dark, lift it out and set aside. Pour in the roulades and marinade. Toss.

6   **MAKE SAUCE**
1 tablespoon sugar
1 tablespoon vinegar
1 cup chicken stock
2 tablespoons orange marmalade

Add sauce ingredients to wok and toss with meat. Keep turning the mixture at high heat until the gravy becomes translucent and bubbles. Serve roulades and sauce with rendered citrus peel sprinkled over top, and accompany with rice or noodles.

*Improvisation not recommended; use all measurements as given.

Rice Crumb Steamed Pork

This is a family recipe, the cornerstone of our New Year's dinner. There is a sensual combination of pork, roasted rice kernels, sweet potatoes, and elusive spices. The recipe is neither difficult nor time consuming, but the marinade must be started the night before and roasting the rice takes 30 minutes.*

SERVES 6 PEOPLE

---

1 **CUT AND MARINATE**
a small Boston butt, about 2½ to 3 pounds
3 tablespoons light soy sauce
1 tablespoon dark soy sauce
⅓ cup rice wine or sherry
½ star anise
1 teaspoon ground cinnamon

Leave fat on the meat and slice butt into pieces ¼ inch thick. Place in a bowl. Pour remaining ingredients over meat. Cover and refrigerate overnight.

---

2 **DRY-FRY**
1 cup white rice
1 cup glutinous rice
½ star anise
½-inch stick of cinnamon

Place rice and spices in a hot, dry wok. Toss at a leisurely pace until they begin to turn brown. Or place rice and spices in a flat pan and put under the broiler, stirring and shaking often to prevent burning. Roast rice, either in wok or in broiler, for 30 minutes. The more slowly you roast the rice, the richer its aroma. Remove and let cool. Remove cinnamon.

---

3 **GRIND**

When roasted rice has cooled, peel anise petals off and discard seeds (you'll use only the pod). Measure ¼ teaspoon of the petals and grind with rice in a food processor or blender until you have a rough crumble. The particles of rice should be visible. Set rice crumbs aside.

---

4 **CUT AND TOSS**
1½ pounds sweet potatoes
½ cup brown sugar

Peel potatoes and slice into ¾-inch-thick pieces. Toss in the brown sugar, then set aside.

184

5 *ASSEMBLE*

Pour the rice crumbs onto a sheet of waxed paper. Choose a 6-cup loaf pan or flared bowl 3 inches deep, and check that it fits under the wok lid. Line the bottom of the mold with sweet potato slices, then pack in the meat, standing pieces on edge. Arrange the remaining potato slices over the top. Steam over high heat for 30 minutes, then reduce to medium-low and cook for 2 hours. Check every 30 minutes and keep a kettle of simmering water nearby to replenish the steaming water.

6 *SERVE*

Check to see if meat is done by slipping a chopstick or spoon handle through the mass to the bottom. If it goes in with ease, invert the steamed cake onto a serving dish and serve immediately.

Improvisation not recommended; use all measurements as given.

Eastern Steak with Culled Vegetables

This is steak with Asian flavorings, very good served over a bed of greens such as Culled Asparagus or Culled Broccoli. But it is best over Chinese mustard greens—greens which are fleshy and succulent, unlike the sharp and pungent American mustard greens. If you can obtain the Chinese greens, prepare them as you would the culled vegetable.

SERVES 4 PEOPLE

1 **CUT AND SEASON**
a 2-pound piece of beef tenderloin or strip or sirloin steak
2 tablespoons soy sauce
1 tablespoon oyster sauce
1 tablespoon sherry
1/2 teaspoon baking soda

Cut meat into 4 steaks, each 5/8 inch thick. Combine soy sauce, oyster sauce, and sherry in a deep dish. Dissolve the baking soda in the seasonings, then lower the steaks into the mixture and rub thoroughly with it. Let meat absorb seasonings for about 15 to 30 minutes.

2 **PREPARE VEGETABLE**
1 recipe Culled Asparagus or Culled Broccoli (without sauce)

Cut vegetables while bringing water to boil in wok, and remove to serving platter. (See page 90 or 91 for procedures to follow in preparing the vegetable.)

3 **FRY**
4 1/4 cups oil
4 teaspoons oyster sauce

As soon as vegetable is done, pour off water and dry the wok. Heat oil in wok over high heat. When oil is hot, add the steaks. Fry over high heat for about 2 minutes on each side if you like them rare, longer if you prefer them better done. Remove steaks from wok and keep warm. Quickly, pour the vegetable—and the little water collected around it—into the wok and stir to heat vegetable and to deglaze the coagulated juices stuck to the side of the wok. You should start to get a little sauce forming in the bottom of the wok. Pour in the oyster sauce a teaspoon at a time until the vegetables are seasoned to your liking.

4 **ARRANGE AND SERVE**

Lay the vegetable on a serving platter, making an attractive bed. Place the steaks on top, scooping remainder of sauce in wok over them, and serve immediately.

Chicken and Prosciutto

PAGE *192*

Chicken and Whole Pesto

PAGE 193

Turkey and Pecans
Kungpao Style

PAGES *194-195*

Veal Roulades
with Orange Peel

PAGE *182*

Ham Rolls with Sweet Potato Mousse

 A light purée of sweet potatoes is rolled into slices of ham. The rolls are served with a quick and light sauce made from the steaming juices of the ham and potatoes.

SERVES 4

---

1 | **PEEL AND CUT**
$1\frac{1}{2}$ *pounds sweet potatoes* | Bring water to a boil in the wok with rack in place. Peel, then slice the sweet potatoes $\frac{1}{2}$ inch thick. Steam on rack or in plate until a fork slips through easily, about 15 minutes. Remove.

---

2 | **PUREE AND SEASON**
$\frac{1}{4}$ *cup butter, softened*
1 egg
$\frac{1}{4}$ *cup chopped dates*
pinch each of ground ginger and nutmeg
1 tablespoon minced candied ginger (optional) | While they are still warm, put the potatoes through a food mill or mash by hand, removing long fibers as you work. Quickly mix in the butter by tablespoons. When mixture has cooled enough to touch, beat in the egg, then stir in the dates and seasonings. Refrigerate until cool, about 15 minutes.

---

3 | **ASSEMBLE**
8 to 10 large slices cooked Polish ham, about $\frac{1}{8}$ *inch thick and 5 to 6 inches wide*
$\frac{1}{4}$ *cup dried currants* | Place 2 heaping tablespoons of the potato mousse onto a slice of ham, and roll ham around filling. Continue with remaining ham slices. Place each finished roll onto a steaming plate, seam side down. Sprinkle rolls with the currants.

---

4 | **STEAM** | Bring water to boil in wok with rack in place. Steam rolls for 10 to 15 minutes.

---

5 | **MAKE SAUCE**
$\frac{1}{4}$ *cup butter*
1 tablespoon rum
2 teaspoons Dijon-type mustard | While the ham is steaming, heat the butter and rum in a small saucepan. When the butter has melted and is bubbling, add the mustard. Keep warm over low heat. When rolls have steamed, lift dish out of wok and drain off cooking juices into butter mixture. Stir gently and then pour the sauce over the rolls. Serve immediately.

Whole Crispy Chicken

The skin of a chicken is a perfect protective coating—a natural robe which retains moisture and slowly bastes the meat within. In this Chinese dish, a whole chicken is plunged in hot oil, and continually doused with ladlefuls of boiling oil. The chicken emerges with a crisp light skin while the flesh underneath remains sweet and succulent. The challenge of this dish lies in coloring the bird with an even and warm brown. The chicken is first steamed to be certain it is thoroughly cooked, then basted with a thin coating of honey and vinegar so that the sugar in the honey fries to a beautiful caramel color, and left to air-dry to rid the skin of moisture. It is served with a wok-roasted herbal salt which should be made in advance.

SERVES 4 PEOPLE

1

STEAM
1 frying chicken,
    about 3 pounds,
    at room
    temperature
1 tablespoon honey
1 tablespoon vinegar

Heat water in wok, with steaming rack in place. Steam chicken for 17 minutes. Near the end of the steaming, mix together the honey and vinegar. When chicken is done, immediately move to a rack and brush honey mixture onto the skin. Let chicken cool for from 6 to 12 hours. Secure bird so it is vertical by hanging it or spearing it on a vertical roasting cone. This allows it to dry more evenly inside and out.

2

DEEP-FRY
5 cups oil

Check wok and be certain there is no moisture present. Add oil and heat to 350 degrees. Insert a metal teaspoon or vertical roasting cone into the cavity of the chicken and slide the chicken into the wok, breast side down. Most of the bird should be submerged. Use the wok ladle to douse the exposed parts of the chicken with the surrounding oil. The thickest parts (thighs and legs) should have oil ladled over them most. Nudge the chicken every so often to make sure no part of it scorches on a hot spot against the wok. Use tongs and carefully turn the chicken after 5 minutes. Bathe the breast side with the oil at a steady pace, especially the lighter colored places. The chicken becomes shiny all over—this takes about 10 minutes. Remove from wok and drain on a rack until cool enough to handle. Cut into 4 pieces and serve with plain rice and roasted salt.

ROAST
2 tablespoons salt
6 sprigs rosemary or
    other herb
½ tablespoon black
    or Sichuan
    peppercorns,
    coarsely ground

Using a dry wok on medium-high heat, toss ingredients at a moderate speed for about 15 minutes. The herbal perfume will soon assail your nostrils and the salt turn a gray-brown. Scoop out and cool.

NOTE: This preparation can be used to make crisp cornish hens as well. The hens are less awkward to fry because they are not as large nor are they as fatty, which means the skin does not emerge quite as tenderly crisp, but they are a good way of practicing before trying the larger bird. Proceed as for the chicken, making sure the hens are at room temperature before you steam them for 10 minutes.

Red Chicken

The red *in the name of this dish refers to both the color of the sauce and to the hotness. This chicken is stir-fried in a paste made from red chilies but, luckily, tomatoes are also included and you can increase the proportion of tomatoes to chilies while maintaining the red color of the dish.**

SERVES 4 PEOPLE

---

1 | **CUT**
10 cloves garlic
10 shallots
½ pound
    mushrooms
1 medium tomato
1 cup (packed) fresh
    holy basil or
    purple basil

Slice garlic and shallots paper thin; you should have ½ cup of each when sliced. Wipe mushrooms, then cut smaller ones in half and larger ones into quarters. Peel tomato and squeeze out seeds, then cut into eighths. Pick the leaves and tops off basil stems.

---

2 | **PUREE**
5 fresh hot red chili
    peppers, seeded
    and sliced
2 tablespoons shrimp
    paste
1 teaspoon salt

Put chili peppers, shrimp paste, and salt into the bowl of a food processor or blender and run the machine until you have a smooth paste, or pound in a mortar until smooth.

---

3 | **CUT AND SEASON**
6 chicken thighs
2 tablespoons sherry

Remove chicken meat from the bones and cut into ½-inch dice. Place in a bowl with the sherry and blend.

---

4 | **FRY**
6 to 8 tablespoons
    oil

Heat oil in wok over high heat, then add the garlic pieces and fry until lightly brown and crisp. Remove with a perforated ladle, then add the shallots and fry until crisp. Remove, leaving oil in wok.

---

5 | **STIR-FRY**

Add the pepper paste to the wok and stir-fry briefly. When fragrant, add the chicken and mushrooms. Drizzle in extra oil if necessary.

---

6 | **COMBINE-FRY**
2 tablespoons tomato
    paste

When the chicken meat turns color and is firm, in about 2 minutes, add the tomato paste. Add the garlic and shallot chips, saving about 1 teaspoon of each to serve as a garnish. Add the tomato, and then add the basil. Give the mixture a few turns to incorporate the leaves, then scoop out.

7 **SERVE**
¹⁄₄ cup oil
additional basil
leaves

Sprinkle with remaining garlic and shallot chips. To prepare garnish, heat oil and add the basil leaves. Give them
2 to 3 tosses while they curl and turn dark, then immediately drizzle the oil and leaves over the chicken. Serve with
plain rice or noodles.

Improvisation not recommended; use all measurements as given.

Chicken and Prosciutto

This dish has the elegance of simplicity: fresh chicken, superb ham, and the lightest touch of seasonings. Then the ever-so-gentle heat of steam binds the natural juices of the ingredients.

SERVES 4 PEOPLE

---

1 **SOAK**
4 to 6 Chinese black mushrooms (optional)

Place mushrooms in a small bowl with cold water and soak until softened, about 30 minutes. Cut stems off flush with the caps.

---

2 **MIX**
4 chicken breast halves, boned but with skin left on
1 tablespoon Madeira wine
2 tablespoons light soy sauce

Mix ingredients in a steaming dish with the mushrooms.

---

3 **STEAM**
4 slices prosciutto, paper thin

Bring water to a boil in wok, with rack in place. Alternate the ham slices and chicken breasts in dish, with ham covering half of each breast and with the breasts just touching each other. The skin side of the chicken should be down. Steam over high heat for 20 to 25 minutes. Check the thickest part of the breast and if no pink juices flow, it is done.

---

4 **SERVE**

Lift steaming plate onto a serving platter and remove the skin from chicken if you wish. Arrange mushrooms attractively over and serve with bread or rice.

Chicken and Whole Pesto

Three elements that go into making Italian pesto—pine nuts, fresh basil, and garlic—remain whole here and are stir-fried with velvety smooth chicken slivers. The initial frying of the chicken may seem to use excessive oil, but the oil is drained off. This oil bath makes the meat sleek in texture, but if you are concerned, instead stir-fry the chicken in ¼ cup oil and forego the glaze. Handle the pine nuts deftly, however. They burn easily in the hot oil and continue to cook once they are taken out. Skim them out with the perforated ladle as soon as they turn a shade darker— within 5 to 10 seconds.*

SERVES 2 PEOPLE

1

CUT
1 whole chicken breast
½ egg white
¼ teaspoon salt
½ tablespoon cornstarch
2 cups packed fresh basil leaves
2 cloves garlic

Remove and discard tendons in the 2 fillets of the chicken breast. (The fillets lie immediately against the crest of the breast bone.) Slice into ⅛-inch pieces, with the grain. Mix egg white with salt and cornstarch, then blend with chicken and refrigerate for 30 minutes. Meanwhile, cut basil leaves into ¼-inch strips across the veins. Cut garlic into 1⁄16-inch slivers.

2

FRY
2 cups oil
1 cup pine nuts

Prepare to drain oil by arranging a strainer over a wide, heatproof container. Heat the oil in the wok to 300 degrees. Add the pine nuts and stir around for 10 seconds. Catch nuts with the perforated ladle and drain on paper towels. Keep the oil at the same 300 degrees, then pour in the chicken mixture all at once and stir vigorously, swilling the chicken in the oil with the perforated spatula or wire scoop, inverted. As soon as the pieces of chicken separate and turn white, about 45 seconds, pour the entire contents of the wok into the strainer.

3

STIR-FRY
1 tablespoon cornstarch mixed with 2½ tablespoons water

Return 1½ tablespoons of oil to the wok and add the garlic slices. Stir-fry until their aroma reaches your nose, then add the chicken from the strainer. Re-stir the cornstarch mixture, then add it to the wok, tossing vigorously. A very light but clear and shiny sauce will coat the pieces. Pour in the basil leaves and toss just until they go limp. Then add the nuts and toss to combine. Remove from wok immediately and serve with bread, rice, or noodles.

*Improvisation not recommended; use all measurements as given.

Turkey and Pecans, Kungpao Style

 The spicy chicken and peanuts dish known as kungpao *has become popular in recent years. In this variation on that favorite, I substitute two truly American ingredients—turkey and pecans. Whole pieces of dried red pepper season the dish, but don't eat them. After their flavor is released in the hot oil, they turn black and are left in for dramatic effect, and this garnish then reminds you of the sting in the dish. Smaller peppers carry more potency, so you may choose to go with the bigger ones for a better visual effect and for fewer burned tongues.**

SERVES 4 PEOPLE

---

1 **PREPARE**
1 to 1½ cups whole dried red peppers
1 to 2 turkey breast fillets, about 1 pound

With your fingers, rip apart the peppers into ½- to 1-inch long pieces. Shake out the seeds. Scrape the ligament off the turkey and cut meat into ⅝-inch dice.

---

2 **SEASON**
2 tablespoons bean paste; or 1½ tablespoons dark soy sauce
1 tablespoon cornstarch
1 egg white

Mash any loose beans into the bean paste, and then combine with remaining ingredients and blend with turkey. Let stand for at least 30 minutes.

---

3 **ASSEMBLE**
1 teaspoon cornstarch
2 tablespoons water
1 tablespoon soy sauce
2 teaspoons vinegar
2 teaspoons sugar

Combine cornstarch with water, soy sauce, vinegar, and sugar in a small bowl. Set aside in a handy spot near stove.

4	**FRY** *4 cups oil* *1 cup shelled pecans,* *large ones broken* *in half*	Place a strainer over a heatproof bowl or saucepan, which will receive the hot oil from the frying. Heat oil in wok and have ready a wire scoop or perforated ladle. When oil is hot, add the pecans. Stir a few times; the pecans will burn easily so do not let them turn darker. As soon as they suggest a new shade, scoop them out. Turn down the heat under the oil and add the turkey. Stir with the inverted spatula and toss vigorously. The pieces will separate and turn white. Lift the wok and pour the contents into the strainer.
5	**STIR-FRY**	Return 6 tablespoons of the oil to the wok and fry the peppers. When they blacken, pour in the turkey and toss. Re-stir the cornstarch mixture and pour into the wok. Turn the mixture rapidly; the liquid will thicken and lightly glaze the turkey. Add the pecans and just turn to combine, then serve immediately with rice.

*Improvisation not recommended; use all measurements as given.

Grilled Spicy Duck

Improperly prepared, duck can be greasy and the skin leathery. In this recipe, how-
ever, the duck is steamed first, rendering out the fat but letting the flavors penetrate.
Then it is grilled, and the result is a very crisp, fragrant skin enveloping a moist
duck.*

SERVES 4 PEOPLE

---

1 | **PREPARE** | If using a frozen duck, allow to thaw. Split the duck down
| 1 duckling, fresh or | its back but just to one side of the backbone. Press duck
| frozen | open, getting it to lie almost flat. Chop the backbone off
| 1 teaspoon salt | altogether, using a cleaver, then rub the duck with salt. Set
| | aside for 2 to 4 hours

---

2 **GRIND**

3 tablespoons
  coriander seeds
1½ tablespoons
  fennel seeds
1 tablespoon cumin
  seeds
1 teaspoon turmeric
½ teaspoon ground
  nutmeg
½ teaspoon mace
½ teaspoon
  cinnamon
½ teaspoon cloves
½ teaspoon
  cardamom pods,
  husked
1½ teaspoons
  ground black
  pepper

Place spices in a food processor or blender and grind until
a powder (or substitute a commercial curry powder, but
check listing of ingredients and be certain there is cinnamon and mace.)

---

3 **BLEND**

2 medium onions,
  chopped
4 slices gingerroot
2 cloves garlic
grated rind of 1
  lemon
juice of ½ lemon
2 hot peppers, seeded
1 cup unsweetened
  coconut milk

Add the onions, ginger, garlic, lemon rind and lemon juice,
hot peppers, and coconut milk to the spices and spin again
until you have a thick paste.

196

4	**MARINATE**	Place duck in a steaming dish. Rub with half the paste, saving the remaining paste for later. Let marinate overnight.
5	**STEAM**	Heat water in wok, with rack in place. Steam the duck at medium heat for 2 hours. Add boiling water to the wok when necessary, then remove and let duck cool thoroughly. Refrigerate overnight, if desired.
6	**GRILL** *1½ to 2 pounds* *sweet potato* *(optional)* *½ cup coconut milk* *(optional)*	Heat coals in an outdoor grill. Rub the duck all over with the remaining spice paste. Grill the duck for about 20 minutes, turning to crisp on both sides. If desired slice sweet potato into pieces ⅝ inch thick and place on grill 10 minutes before serving; baste with coconut milk as slices grill.
7	**SERVE**	Cut duck into 4 pieces and serve, accompanied by a crisp stir-fried vegetable and grilled sweet potato slices, if desired.

Improvisation not recommended; use all measurements as given.

Thai Crisp Vermicelli

Called meegrob, *this is a delightful dish that transforms ordinary rice vermicelli into an airy mass of spun-gold threads, with an almost caramelized savory sauce. The Thais serve it as a side dish for curry, but it also works very well as a main course. The sauce can be done a day in advance but then soak the vermicelli, deep-fry, and combine with sauce just before serving.*

SERVES 2 TO 3 AS A MAIN COURSE

---

1 **PREPARE GARNISH**
1 lime
1 fresh hot red
    pepper
fresh coriander
    leaves

Cut 4 paper-thin slices off the lime. Stack the slices and cut the rounds through the center into 8 segments. Seed the pepper and slice very thin. Pinch off tender, small individual leaves of coriander. Set aside.

---

2 **CUT**
4 cloves garlic
4 shallots
¼ to ½ pound
    boneless pork
¼ cup medium
    peeled shrimp

Chop the garlic and shallots; you should have 2 tablespoons of each. Mince or grind the pork. Devein the shrimp and dice.

---

3 **SOFTEN**
3 ounces rice
    vermicelli

About 30 minutes before cooking, spray the noodles with water or plunge them into a sinkful of water. Take them out immediately and fling off the excess moisture. The idea is to just coat them with moisture; the noodles will absorb this external moisture.

---

4 **STIR-FRY**
¼ cup oil,
    approximately
2 tablespoons bean
    paste
2 eggs
1 tablespoon cider
    vinegar
1 tablespoon fish
    sauce
1½ tablespoons
    confectioners
    sugar
¼ teaspoon salt

Heat the oil in the wok over high heat. When oil is hot, add the garlic and shallots and toss until fragrant. Add the meat and shrimp and toss until cooked, about 5 minutes. Add the bean paste and turn it in at a leisurely pace, then add the eggs, 1 at a time, incorporating each into the mixture. Add more oil if the mixture becomes too dry and starts to stick to wok. Continue to turn the contents until all the liquid is evaporated, about 5 minutes. Then pour in the vinegar, fish sauce, confectioners sugar, and salt. Patiently turn the mixture until the sauce becomes sticky as the sugar caramelizes, about 10 minutes. Scoop out. (You can even refrigerate it overnight.) Rinse wok.

5 DEEP-FRY
4 cups oil

Heat oil in wok to 350 degrees. When ready, ease in half the noodles. They will puff to triple their original volume and turn golden instantly. Take out and drain. Deep-fry the rest, then pour out the oil.

6 COMBINE-FRY

Re-heat the meat mixture in the wok. Turn until very hot, then add the crisp noodles. They will break up a little but be gentle to avoid their crumbling completely. Turn only enough to coat them with the meat mixture, and remove from wok. Serve vermicelli garnished with lime and pepper, and top with coriander leaves.

Desserts

These sweets are cooked in the wok as are other foods—by steaming, deep-frying, and occasionally "frying," as in the Chocolate Omelette. The normal Chinese household wok is not expected to produce a dessert on the heels of a complete meal. Moreover, in Chinese cuisine, sweets are intended for teatime—mid-morning or mid-afternoon—or at a brunch, such as dim sum. The problem is not that it is so much to have the wok produce course after course, but it is a great deal too much to ask of an average cook who is also the host of her dinner party.

A few desserts do exploit the last-minute agility that the wok offers—the Chocolate and Almond Cream Omelettes, for instance, and the Chocolate Raspberry Pudding are best when they come piping hot and meltingly tender from the hot wok to the table. Others in this chapter are cooked in advance and served cold, anytime you wish. Finally deep-fried desserts such as the Sweet Rice Balls can be tender and aromatic. Since proportions are extremely important to the texture of these desserts, closely follow the measurements given in the recipes.

Chocolate Omelette

This dessert omelette amounts to a soufflé cooked on the top of the stove. It is easier to make in a widely flared wok than a deep one, and your first few attempts may not be beautiful and tidy, but you can hide the flaws with whipped cream. The omelette will be soft in the middle, flowing out onto the plate.

SERVES 4 PEOPLE

1 **BEAT**
4 eggs, separated
5 tablespoons
granulated sugar
1 teaspoon vanilla
extract
1 tablespoon
all-purpose flour
¼ teaspoon baking
powder

Whip the egg yolks, ¼ cup sugar, and the vanilla until lemony. Stir in the flour and baking powder and set aside. In another bowl, whip the egg whites until they begin to foam. Add the remaining tablespoon of sugar and whip until they form stiff peaks.

2 **FOLD**

Fold about ¼ of the whites into the yolk mixture, then fold in the remainder.

3 **FRY**
6 tablespoons
unsalted butter
¾ cup chopped
semisweet
chocolate or
semisweet morsels

Place wok on medium-high heat. Add half the butter and let melt. Swirl wok so the butter coats the sides. Just before it begins to brown, spoon half the omelette mixture into the wok. Immediately turn heat to medium-low and spread mixture so it is ¾ inch thick. Sprinkle with half the chocolate bits and cover for 30 seconds. Lift the omelette a little; it should begin to set—if not, cover for 30 more seconds. Uncover wok and fold omelette in half or into thirds. Keep folding the soft batter toward the center if it seeps out of sides. Remove to a warmed dish and make second omelette with remaining butter and batter, sprinkling in the remaining chocolate and turning as before.

4 **SERVE**
whipped cream,
flavored with
sugar and vanilla
(optional)

Serve omelettes immediately, with whipped cream.

Almond Cream Omelette

Here is a recipe for an almond-rum cream which is folded into a sweet omelette. Make extra and use it to prepare the Almond Shortcake, too (page 214). The cream will store for up to two weeks in the refrigerator.

SERVES 4 PEOPLE

1 GRIND
2 ounces blanched almonds, about 2/3 cup
1/2 cup confectioners sugar

In a food processor or blender, blend the almonds and confectioners sugar until you have a fine powder. Scrape the bottom and sides of the bowl as you grind the nuts.

2 COMBINE
1/4 pound unsalted butter
1 tablespoon cornstarch
1 egg
2 tablespoons rum

In a bowl, cream the butter until smooth and then add the cornstarch and blend well. Add the egg and blend until incorporated. Add the rum and the almond powder. Mix well. This is the almond cream.

3 BEAT
4 eggs, separated
5 tablespoons granulated sugar
1 tablespoon all-purpose flour
1/4 teaspoon baking powder

In a bowl, whip the egg yolks and 1/4 cup sugar until lemony. Stir in the flour and baking powder and set aside. In another bowl, whip egg whites until they begin to foam. Add the remaining tablespoon of sugar and whip until they form stiff peaks.

4 FOLD

Fold about 1/4 of the whites into the yolk mixture, then fold in the remainder.

5 FRY
6 tablespoons unsalted butter

Place wok on medium-high heat. Add half the butter and let melt. Swirl wok so the butter coats the sides. Just before it begins to brown, spoon half the omelette mixture into the wok. Immediately turn heat to low and spread mixture so it is 3/4 inch thick. Spread with half the almond cream and cover for 30 seconds—longer if it is not well set. Uncover wok and fold omelette in half or into thirds. Keep folding the soft batter toward the center if it seeps out. Remove to a warmed plate and make second omelette with remaining batter, butter, and cream. Serve immediately.

Chocolate Omelette

PAGE 201

Apple Sherbet
with Apple Custard

PAGES 206-207

Steamed Coconut Cream Custard

Coconut custard is a delicate dessert suggesting tropical fragrances and textures, but it must be made with fresh coconut milk and preferably also with palm sugar (see Ingredients). It goes especially well with poached bananas on the side (following recipe).

SERVES 4 PEOPLE

1 **COOK**
1 cup coconut milk, preferably fresh
2 eggs
1/4 cup palm sugar; or 1/2 cup brown sugar

Combine ingredients in a small saucepan set over very low heat and stir, breaking up the palm sugar. The mixture will thicken as the sugar dissolves. Do not beat the mixture for the smoothest results; just stir slowly and patiently as the mixture cooks for 20 to 30 minutes or until it coats a spoon. Pour custard into steaming plate.

2 **STEAM**

Heat water in the wok, with rack in place. Bring water to a simmer, then place custard onto steaming rack and steam over low heat until set—about 20 to 30 minutes. When a tester comes out clean, custard is done. Serve warm or cooled.

Poached Bananas with Coconut Cream

For a substantial dessert, accompany the custard of the preceding recipe with these bananas poached in coconut cream. Or serve the bananas with vanilla ice cream.

SERVES 4 PEOPLE

POACH
4 firm, ripe bananas
2 cups coconut cream

Cut bananas in half, then split each half lengthwise. Simmer the coconut cream in a stainless-steel saucepan or wok. Add the bananas and poach for 10 to 15 minutes. Serve warm, with Coconut Cream Custard, if desired.

Chocolate Raspberry Pudding

 This is a hybrid pudding-soufflé, which is steamed in the wok and served warm. When cooled, it can be cut up and served with ice cream. Only a minimal amount of flour goes into the mix, so it is very tender. The pastry cream, which is made first, is twice what's needed; use the remainder to make the Almond Shortcake (page 214).

SERVES 4 PEOPLE

1 **BOIL**
2 cups milk
1 teaspoon vanilla
 extract
1/2 cup granulated
 sugar

In a large saucepan, combine milk, vanilla, and sugar. It must come to a rolling boil. Keep hot.

2 **WHIP**
6 eggs, separated
3/4 cup granulated
 sugar
2 tablespoons
 all-purpose flour
2 tablespoons
 cornstarch

While milk mixture is warming, beat the egg yolks until they are lemon colored and have gained body. (Leave the whites out at room temperature.) Add the flour and cornstarch to the yolks, then pour 1/3 of the boiling milk into the mixture, whisking continuously. Then pour in remaining milk and return the mixture to the saucepan. Bring to a boil over medium heat, stirring all the while with a whisk to prevent lumps from forming. Count 30 seconds after it first bubbles, then remove from heat. Immediately pour pudding into a shallow jelly roll pan and cover with plastic wrap so skin will form. Let cool or refrigerate overnight. This is the pastry cream.

3 **BUTTER AND COAT**
1 tablespoon
 unsalted butter
1/3 cup raspberry jam

Butter a 8- to 9-inch shallow dish. Spread with the jam.

4 **MELT/PRE-STEAM**
1 cup chopped
 semisweet
 chocolate or
 morsels

Bring water in wok to a boil, with rack in place. Place chocolate on a small dish over the heating water; it will soften and melt.

5 **WHIP**
1/2 cup granulated
 sugar

Beat egg whites at medium speed until they are frothy. Add 1 tablespoon of the sugar, then gradually add the rest as you continue to beat the whites. They will acquire more volume and begin to stiffen. Beat until they form stiff peaks.

6	**COMBINE**	Transfer half of the custard mixture to a mixing bowl. Remove and stir the chocolate, but don't turn the heat off under the wok. Whisk the melted chocolate into the custard; fold in ⅓ of the whites, then fold in the remainder. Pile mixture onto the buttered dish, but no higher than 1½ inches.
7	**STEAM**	Place plate onto steaming rack in wok and steam over high heat for 15 minutes. Do not lift the lid to peek—the soufflé will collapse. After 15 minutes, test soufflé to see if cooked in center, then immediately serve on warmed plates.

Apple Sherbet with Apple Custard

 This dessert contrasts a warm apple custard with a scoop of cold apple sherbet. The custard may be made in advance, then reheated when ready to serve. The sherbet can be made several days earlier and kept frozen.

SERVES 4 PEOPLE

1	**STIR-FRY** 1 jar (28 ounces) apple sauce ¾ cup sugar	Combine apple sauce with sugar in wok and heat over medium heat. Patiently turn and fold the mixture for about 20 minutes. It will at first become watery, then will begin to firm up. Continue turning until the mixture begins to hold its shape, like soft mashed potatoes. It will darken slightly.
2	**COOL AND FREEZE**	Allow sherbet to cool, then transfer to a 4-cup container and freeze for at least 3 hours or until firm.
3	**PEEL AND SLICE** 2 crisp apples, preferably Golden Delicious	Peel apples and slice into 10 to 12 segments. Arrange in 1 layer on a buttered steaming or shallow baking dish.
4	**HEAT** 1½ cups heavy cream; or ¾ cup each *evaporated milk and whole milk* 1 teaspoon vanilla extract ⅓ cup granulated sugar	Place ingredients in saucepan and bring to a rolling boil. Keep hot.
5	**WHIP** 2 eggs ⅓ cup granulated sugar	While milk or cream mixture heats, beat eggs with sugar until lemon colored and thick. Add hot milk to eggs gradually, whisking constantly until well blended.

6 STEAM Bring water to a boil in the wok, with rack in place. Pour custard mixture over the sliced apples and place dish on steaming rack. Steam over medium-low heat for 30 minutes, or until the custard is set. Add hot water to the wok if necessary. When done, remove dish and pour off excess water that might have collected over the custard. Set aside.

7 SERVE When ready to serve, offer custard on individual plates and serve with a scoop of sherbet over it. The idea is for the sherbet to slightly melt.

Snow-topped Cream

This is the classic French dessert oeufs à la neige: *clouds of meringue served atop a custard sauce. Both the meringues and the sauce can be made in advance, so this lovely dessert is a suitably light finale for a large meal.*

SERVES 4 PEOPLE

1 **WHIP**
6 egg whites
¼ cup granulated sugar

Leave whites at room temperature overnight if possible. Whip at medium speed and when they begin to hold their shape, sprinkle in the sugar and continue to beat on low speed for 30 seconds or until stiff peaks form.

2 **POACH**

Heat water in wok to a slight simmer. Have a damp towel on a flat tray close to the wok. Scoop the meringues by tablespoonfuls into the barely simmering water. Do 4 to 5 at a time; they will expand in the water. Turn after 7 minutes, then cook another 3 minutes. Remove the meringues with a slotted spoon onto the towel and let cool while you prepare the remainder. (You could also spiral the meringues out of a pastry bag fitted with a large star tip onto a piece of wet paper, then slide the roses into the simmering water.) Place meringues in refrigerator until you are ready to serve.

3 **BOIL**
2 cups milk
1 teaspoon vanilla extract
½ teaspoon almond extract

Bring milk, vanilla, and almond extract to a boil in a large saucepan. Keep hot.

4 **WHIP AND COMBINE**
4 tablespoons granulated sugar
6 egg yolks

While milk heats, whip sugar and egg yolks until lemon colored and creamy. When the milk boils vigorously, pour it gradually into the whipped yolks, whisking all the time. Return custard to the saucepan and cook over low heat, stirring constantly; the mixture must not boil. When it coats the spoon, in about 15 minutes, let cool, then refrigerate.

5 **SERVE**

Place the custard sauce in a shallow serving bowl with a wide surface area. Float the meringues on top and then serve 1 island per person, spooning the sauce over and around it. If desired, serve with lace cookies, macaroons, or palmiers.

Poached Pears with Hard Sauce

 These are sugar-stuffed pears in a creamy whiskey sauce.

SERVES 4 PEOPLE

1 **PEEL AND CORE**
4 firm pears
1/2 lemon

Cutting only about 2 inches deep, core the pears with an apple or zucchini corer. Do not cut through to the bottom. Peel, then rub the pears with a cut lemon half and place on a steaming dish.

2 **STUFF**
1/3 to 1/2 cup brown
sugar
1/4 cup whiskey
2 vanilla beans, cut
in half

Pack the sugar into each of the pears, then pour in the whiskey. Stick a half a vanilla bean into the brown sugar—it should resemble the stem.

3 **STEAM**

Bring water in wok to a boil, with rack in place. Steam pears for 30 to 45 minutes, or until they are tender throughout. Add water to the wok when necessary and test pears by putting a knife through to the middle.

4 **PREPARE SAUCE**
1 cup confectioners
sugar
1/3 cup butter,
softened
1/4 cup whiskey; or 1
teaspoon vanilla
extract
1/2 cup heavy cream
1 egg yolk

Pour the liquid that forms around the pears into a small saucepan. Boil and reduce it by half, then remove from the heat. Stir in the sugar and butter. When smooth, add the whiskey, the cream, and the egg yolk. Blend well. Place pears on individual plates and pour the sauce over and around each. Serve warm or cold.

Blueberry Pudding

 This is a convenient dessert that takes only five minutes to assemble, easily steamed in the wok.

SERVES 4 PEOPLE

1 **COMBINE**
3 cups fresh or
   frozen blueberries
$^1/_2$ cup granulated
   sugar

Butter a shallow 4-cup steaming or baking dish. Toss the blueberries with the sugar in the dish. The blueberries should almost fill the dish.

2 **MIX**
$^3/_4$ cup all-purpose
   flour
$^1/_2$ tablespoon baking
   powder
2 eggs
$^1/_4$ cup milk
1 teaspoon vanilla
   extract

Quickly combine the flour with the remaining ingredients. Do not overmix; mixture may be lumpy, but that's all right.

3 **STEAM**
2 tablespoons butter

Bring water to a boil in wok, with steaming rack in place. Pour batter over the berries and then dot with butter. Steam over high heat for 20 minutes. If necessary, add boiling water to wok if level goes down.

4 **SERVE**
ice cream

Serve warm or cold, with a spoon. It will be juicy in the center if served warm and is especially good with ice cream.

Sweet Rice Balls

 One or two of these hefty Chinese sweets are more than enough; they are more of a snack than a dessert. It is the glutinous rice flour that gives them their particular texture, at once both custardy and taffylike. Once you've mastered the plain balls, you may wish to make the peanut- or sesame-filled balls.

SERVES 6 TO 8

1 **MIX**
2 cups glutinous rice flour
½ cup confectioners sugar
⅔ cup boiling water

Place flour and sugar in bowl and, while stirring, pour in *vigorously* boiling water. Keep stirring until it is cool enough to handle and then knead on an oiled surface until the dough is smooth and malleable. Form into balls ¾ inch in diameter; you will have about 12 balls.

2 **DEEP-FRY**
½ cup sesame seeds
6 cups oil
confectioners sugar

Heat oil in wok to 350 degrees. As oil heats, dip each ball into water and then roll in sesame seeds. Fry 3 to 4 balls at a time over medium heat. They will expand; cook until they are golden brown, then remove and drain. Serve warm dusted with confectioners sugar.

PEANUT- OR SESAME-FILLED RICE BALLS

1 **MIX**
1 cup peanut butter, preferably crunchy or homemade; or tahini paste
¼ cup granulated sugar

Mix peanut butter or tahini paste with sugar.

2 **FORM**

Take a piece of rice ball dough and flatten it with the palm of your hand. Place a rounded tablespoon of filling in the middle and pinch to seal. Roll between the palms of your hands to round off, then deep-fry as for plain sweet rice balls.

Cannoli with Chestnut Cream

I have taken great liberties with this Italian favorite. Here I use fresh eggroll or wonton wrappers as the pastry and fill them with a chestnut cream lightened with whipped cream.

SERVES 10 PEOPLE

1 **DEEP-FRY**
2 cups oil
20 wonton wrappers

Heat oil in wok to 350 degrees. Wrap the wonton wrappers around cannoli forms and seal by painting a fingertip of water across the edge of the pastry. Fry wrappers until golden blond. If using eggroll wrappers, trim them a little to fit cannoli forms. Remove pastries from the forms and let cool.

2 **WHIP**
1 cup heavy cream
¼ cup granulated
  sugar
1 tablespoon rum

Have the cream cold. Whip at medium speed gradually adding the sugar as the cream gains body. Add the rum and blend.

3 **FLAVOR AND STUFF**
½ cup chestnut
  purée
½ cup tiny semisweet
  morsels

Add the chestnut purée and chocolate morsels to the cream. Stuff mixture into the pastries using a pastry bag if you wish. Serve very soon, or the filling will soften the crusts.

Upside-down Lemon Cheesecake

 A classic lemon butter is layered beneath a cheesecake. When inverted, the butter is cooked, coating the cheesecake with a shimmering, tart glaze.

SERVES 6 TO 8 PEOPLE

1 **CREAM AND MIX**
1 pound cream cheese
¾ cup granulated sugar
½ teaspoon vanilla extract
½ teaspoon lemon juice
2 eggs

Using an electric mixer, whip cream cheese with sugar until totally dissolved. Add the vanilla and lemon juice, mix; then incorporate the eggs 1 at a time with the mixer set on slow speed. Do not beat vigorously—stop as soon as the eggs are blended in.

2 **COMBINE**
⅛ teaspoon grated lemon rind
3 tablespoons lemon juice
¾ cup confectioners sugar
1 tablespoon unsalted butter, melted
3 egg yolks

Place lemon rind, juice, sugar, and melted butter in a small bowl, then whisk in the yolks. This is the lemon butter.

3 **ASSEMBLE AND STEAM**

Heat water in wok with steaming rack in place. Generously butter a steaming plate—4-cup capacity—or an 8-inch shallow cake pan. Pour the lemon butter into the bottom and rotate so that bottom is coated with the mixture. Immediately pour in the cream cheese mixture and place on steaming rack in wok. Steam over low heat for 30 to 40 minutes or until a tester comes out clean.

4 **SERVE**

Remove cake from rack and let cool. Run a spatula around edges and across bottom as much as possible. Then unmold onto a serving platter. A layer of the lemon butter will remain attached to the pan—this can't be helped—but the rest will top the cheesecake like a glaze. Refrigerate and serve chilled.

Almond Shortcake with Candied Pumpkin

 This cake comes as close as possible to marzipan without the assertive candylike aroma or texture. It says "almond" but is still a buttery cake, and it is best made the day before serving.

SERVES 4 TO 6 PEOPLE

1 | **COMBINE**
1 recipe Almond Cream (page 202)
1/2 recipe Pastry Cream (page 204) | Combine the almond cream and pastry cream and pour into a buttered 4-cup steaming dish or ceramic pie plate. Cover loosely with foil to give the cake room to puff up.

2 | **STEAM** | Bring water to a boil in wok, with rack in place. Steam cake over medium-high heat for 45 minutes to 1 hour, or until a tester comes out clean. Add hot water to wok when necessary. Cool thoroughly and refrigerate overnight.

3 | **BOIL**
2 cups water
2 cups granulated sugar
2 tablespoons light corn syrup | Bring water, sugar, and corn syrup to a boil in a heavy saucepan and stir until the sugar crystals are melted. Cook over high heat until syrup thickens, about 10 minutes.

4 | **CUT AND COOK**
1 small pumpkin or winter squash | Peel pumpkin and cut lengthwise into 1/2-inch-wide slices that are 3 inches long. Use about 2 cups of slices. Cook in the syrup over high heat until pumpkin pieces turn clear. Drain and store, covered, in refrigerator.

5 | **SERVE** | When ready to serve cake, cut into thin slices and decorate with candied pumpkin.

Conversion Tables

The following are conversion tables and other information applicable to those converting the recipes in this book for use in other English-speaking countries. The cup and spoon measures given in this book are U.S. Customary; use these tables when working with British Imperial or Metric kitchen utensils.

LIQUID MEASURES

The old Imperial pint is larger than the U.S. pint; therefore note the following when measuring the liquid ingredients.

U.S.	Imperial
1 cup = 8 fluid ounces	1 cup = 10 fluid ounces
½ cup = 4 fluid ounces	½ cup = 5 fluid ounces
1 tablespoon = ¾ fluid ounce	1 tablespoon = 1 fluid ounce

U.S. Measure	Metric	Imperial*
1 quart	946 ml	1½+ pints
1 pint	473 ml	¾+ pint
1 cup	236 ml	−½ pint
1 tablespoon	15 ml	−1 tablespoon
1 teaspoon	5 ml	−1 teaspoon

WEIGHT AND VOLUME MEASURES

U.S. cooking procedures usually measure certain items by volume, although in the Metric or Imperial systems they are measured by weight. Here are some approximate equivalents for basic items.*

	U.S. Customary	Metric	Imperial
Apples (peeled and sliced)	3 cups	500 g	1 pound
Butter	½ cup	125 g	4 ounces
	1 tablespoon	15 g	½ ounce
Cheese (grated)	½ cup	60 g	2 ounces
Flour, all-purpose (sifted)	1 cup	128 g	4¼ ounces
	½ cup	60 g	2⅛ ounces
Herbs, fresh	2 tablespoons chopped	7 g	¼ ounce
Mushrooms, fresh (chopped)	4 cups	300 g	10 ounces
Peas, fresh (shelled)	1 cup	450 g	1 pound
Raisins (or Sultanas)	¾ cup	125 g	4 ounces
Rice	1 cup (raw)	225 g	8 ounces
	3 cups (cooked)	225 g	8 ounces
Sugar (granulated)	1 cup	240 g	8 ounces
	½ cup	120 g	4 ounces
	¼ cup	60 g	2 ounces
	1 tablespoon	15 g	½ ounce
Tomatoes, fresh (peeled, seeded, juiced)	1½ cups	450 g	1 pound

*Note that exact quantities cannot always be given. Differences are more crucial when dealing with larger quantities. For teaspoon and tablespoon measures, simply use scant quantities, or for more accurate conversions rely upon metric measures.

OVEN TEMPERATURES

Gas Mark	¼	2	4	6	8
Fahrenheit	225	300	350	400	450
Celsius	107	150	178	205	233

Index